PLUTARCH

D.A. Russell

Second Edition
Foreword and Bibliography by Judith Mossman

BRISTOL CLASSICAL PAPERBACKS

First published in 1972 by Gerald Duckworth & Co. Ltd

This edition published in 2001 by
Bristol Classical Press
an imprint of
Gerald Duckworth & Co. Ltd
61 Frith Street
London W1D 3JL
e-mail: inquiries@duckworth-publishers.co.uk
Website: www.ducknet.co.uk

© 1972, 2001 D.A. Russell

A catalogue record for this book is available
from the British Library

ISBN 1-85399-620-3

Printed in Great Britain by
Booksprint

Contents

PLVTARQVE.

Ta fage inftruction fert de riche couronne
A Trajan, efleué par deffus tous humains.
Si les grands te portoient au cœur & dans leurs mains,
Vertu viuroit au lieu de Venus & Bellone

Medallion of Plutarch, with verses by Simon Goulart, from *Les hommes illustres grecs et romains*, translated from the Greek by Jacques Amyot, published by Frederic Leonard, Paris, 1655.

Foreword

When Donald Russell's *Plutarch* was first published in 1972, he wrote in his preface 'There has been a great deal of scholarly work on Plutarch in recent years, especially in France'. Yet this book was very different from most other contemporary books on Plutarch, however valuable. Neither Jones nor Wardman, nor Babut, despite their many excellent qualities, influenced subsequent scholarship to quite the same extent.[1] Russell's treatment was so wide-ranging, extending the same sympathetic understanding to *Lives* and *Moralia* alike; his analysis of Plutarch's style revealed so much about the fine literary qualities of works which most were accustomed to quarry for source material rather than read as sophisticated and artful texts; and his discussion of Plutarch's *Nachleben* and his comparison of some of his translators drew attention further to the high narrative art which had rarely been accorded detailed criticism or analysis by scholars. Russell's own elegant and pleasing style added to the attractions of the book.

Since it appeared, *very* much more work has been done on Plutarch, and not only in France. The following bibliography, lightly annotated, is an attempt to catalogue some of the main developments from the publication of Russell's book to the present. It is not intended to be comprehensive, but it will be clear, even from a partial survey, that much of what has been done over the last thirty years could not have been attempted without the inspiration of Russell's book, or, in many cases, his personal contribution as a teacher, supervisor or advisor. Our part of the global scholarly community owes him a great deal.

TEXTS

The Budé edition of the *Lives* and *Moralia* is now complete. Several Italian series of annotated texts and translations of the *Lives* are in

---

[1] D. Babut, *Plutarque et le stoicisme*, Paris; C. P. Jones, *Plutarch and Rome*, Oxford; A. Wardman, *Plutarch's Lives*, London.

progress: one published in Milan by the Fondazione Lorenzo Valla, others, also published in Milan, by Rizzoli, and by Garzanti, and one published in Turin. A series of commentaries on the *Moralia* has also appeared and continues to proceed, published in Naples.

TRANSLATIONS

Lives

In addition to the Penguin translations, which are not yet quite complete, there are now two selections of Greek and Roman *Lives* translated by Robin Waterfield for Oxford World's Classics, with extremely useful introductions, bibliography and notes by Philip Stadter (1998 and 1999). Wordsworth Classics of World Literature have also produced a volume of selected pairs of *Lives* in Sir Thomas North's translation, introduced by Judith Mossman (1998).

Moralia

Robin Waterfield has translated selections from the *Moralia* for Penguin (1992); Russell produced another selection for Oxford World's Classics, now unfortunately out of print (1993). There is a series of Italian translations of some of the treatises, under the supervision of Dario del Corno, published by the Adelphi 'Piccola Biblioteca'.

ANNOTATED EDITIONS OF INDIVIDUAL WORKS

Some of the best recent work available has been published in this format, which perhaps suits the wide range of much of Plutarch's writing. Apart from the Italian series mentioned above, many *Lives* have been edited separately:

Themistocles, ed. F. J. Frost, Princeton 1980.

Cicero, ed. J. L. Moles, Warminster 1988.

Antony, ed. Christopher Pelling, Cambridge 1988.

Cimon, ed. A. Blamire, London 1989.

Aristides and Cato, ed. D. Sansone, Warminster 1989.

Pericles, ed. P. A. Stadter, Chapel Hill 1989.

Sertorius, ed. C. F. Konrad, Chapel Hill 1994.

Agesilaos, ed. D. R. Shipley, Oxford 1997.

Of these, it seems worth picking out Moles, Pelling and Stadter as

being particularly concerned with the literary merits and over-
arching structure of the *Lives*. Although technically commentaries
on individual texts, each contributes more to the reader's understanding of the author as a whole than just the elucidation of one
work.

Moralia

De audiendo, ed. B. P. Hillyard 1981.

Quaestiones Convivales (three volumes), ed. S-T. Theodorsson, Göteborg
    1989, 1990, 1996.

De Pythiae oraculis, ed. S. Schröder, 1990.

Coniugalia Praecepta and Consolatio ad uxorem, ed. S. Pomeroy, Oxford
    1999.

De Herodoti malignitate, ed. Anthony Bowen, Warminster 1992.

Many of the *Moralia* remain less studied than they deserve, though
there is work in progress on this area.

BOOKS AND ARTICLES

Here, too, much fine work has been done recently on a variety of
aspects of Plutarch's writing and thought:

Monographs

F. E. Brenk, *In Mist Apparelled*, Leiden 1977.

Y. Vernière, *Symboles et Mythes dans la pensée de Plutarque*, Paris 1977.

F. Le Corsu, *Plutarque et les femmes dans les* Vies parallèles, Paris 1981.

G. J. D. Aalders, *Plutarch's Political Thought*, Amsterdam 1982.

B. Gentili and G. Cerri, *History and Biography in Ancient Thought*,
    Amsterdam 1988.

L. van der Stockt, *Twinkling and Twilight: Plutarch's reflections on literature*,
    Brussels 1992.

F. Frazier, *Histoire et morale dans les* Vies parallèles *de Plutarque*, Paris
    1996.

Tim Duff, *Plutarch's* Lives: *Exploring Virtue and Vice*, Oxford 1999.

There are many collections of essays on Plutarch, often consisting
of, or selecting from, the *Acta* of the many conferences on Plutarch
held by the genial and active International Plutarch Society, whose
journal, *Ploutarchos*, edited by Frances B. Titchener, does excellent

work in keeping scholars up to date with the progress of international scholarship on Plutarch. The following is just a selection, and
rather an Anglophone one at that.

Collections of articles

Aufstieg und Niedergang der römischen Welt 2. 33. 6 contains a range of
articles on Plutarch in a variety of languages.

F. E. Brenk and I. Gallo, eds, *Miscellanea Plutarchea (Atti del I convegno
di studi su Plutarco, Roma, 23 novembre 1985, Quaderni del Giornale
Filologico Ferrarese* 8, Ferrara 1986.

P. A. Stadter, ed., *Plutarch and the Historical Tradition*, London 1992.

B. Scardigli, ed., *Essays on Plutarch's Lives*, Oxford 1995.

J. A. Fernandez Delgado and F. Pordomingo Pardo, eds, *Estudios
sobre Plutarco IV. Aspectos Formales*, Madrid 1996.

L. van der Stockt, *Plutarchea Lovaniensia*, Leuven 1996.

J. M. Mossman, ed., *Plutarch and his Intellectual World*, Swansea 1997.

L. van der Stockt, ed., *Rhetorical Theory and Praxis in Plutarch*, Leuven
2000.

Christopher Pelling, *Plutarch and History: Eighteen Studies*, Swansea 2002.

Of these, Scardigli usefully collects and reprints a number of
articles from various sources, and introduces them with an excellent
bibliographical essay. The final volume on the list, Christopher
Pelling's collected essays, will be particularly helpful for the reader
seeking a range of insights into Plutarch's biographical writings.
Pelling's approach, influenced in a number of respects by Russell,
successfully combines the best skills of the literary critic and the
ancient historian, to impressive effect.

Other articles (a very small and rather arbitrary selection of pieces
not so far reprinted, as far as I am aware):

F. H. Sandbach, 'Plutarch and Aristotle', *ICS* 7.2 (1982), 207-32.

J. Geiger, 'Nepos and Plutarch: From Latin to Greek Political
Biography', *ICS* 13 (1988), 245-56.

Aristoula Georgiadou, 'The *Lives of the Caesars* and Plutarch's other
Lives', *ICS* 13.2 (1988), 349-56.

David Larmour, 'Plutarch's compositional methods in the *Theseus*
and *Romulus*' *TAPA* 118 (1988), 361-75.

J. de Romilly, 'Rencontres avec Plutarque', *ICS* 13.2 (1988), 219-29.

Simon Swain, 'Character Change in Plutarch', *Phoenix* 43 (1989), 62-8.

——'Plutarch: Chance, Providence and History', *AJP* 110 (1989), 272-302.

——'Plutarchan Synkrisis', *Eranos* 90 (1992), 101-11.

[a small sample of a very impressive output].

T. Saunders, '*De sera numinis vindicta* in the tradition of Greek penology', *Studi Economici-Giuridici* 54 (1991-2), 65-94.

D. Braund, 'Dionysiac Tragedy in Plutarch, *Crassus*', *CQ* 43 (1993), 468-74.

John Marincola, 'Plutarch's Refutation of Herodotus', *AncW* 25 (1994), 191-203.

S. Dusanic, 'Plato and Plutarch's Fictional Techniques: the Death of the Great Pan', *RhM* 139 (1996), 276-94.

W. J. Tatum, 'The Regal Image in Plutarch's *Lives*', *JHS* 106 (1996), 135-51.

Alexei Zadorozhnyy, 'Tragedy and Epic in Plutarch's *Crassus*', *Hermes* 125 (1997), 169-82.

Electronic journals have also begun to publish material on Plutarch: see especially *Histos* (http://www.dur.ac.uk/Classics/histos), which has articles on Plutarch in all of its first three volumes.

CULTURAL CONTEXT

This has if anything become more important since the 1970s, with the proliferation of interest in post-colonialism and the rise in the study of some of Plutarch's formerly neglected contemporaries such as Dio. A few of the most important recent contributions include:

S. Alcock, *Graecia Capta: the Landscapes of Roman Greece*, Cambridge 1993.

M. W. Gleeson, *Making Men: Sophists and Self-Presentation in Ancient Rome*, Princeton 1995.

Simon Swain, *Hellenism and Empire: Language, Classicism and Power in the Greek World*, Oxford 1996 (especially pp. 135-86 on Plutarch).

INFLUENCE

This too has been an area of expansion, particularly in regard to Plutarch and Shakespeare. Apart from Pelling's excellent remarks on this topic in his edition of the *Antony* (see above), and the reprinting of selections from North's translation by Wordsworth (see above) the following may also be of interest:

J. M. Mossman, '*Henry V* and Plutarch's *Alexander*', *Shakespeare Quarterly* 45. 1 (1994), 57-73.

M. A. McGrail, ed., *Shakespeare's Plutarch (Poietica* 48), Tokyo 1997.

Preface

Plutarch's *Lives* and *Morals* are among the formative books of western civilisation. Written around A.D. 100, in Greece under Roman rule, they reflect the conditions of that time: not only the political limitations, but—more important—the rich inheritance of post-classical as well as classical Greek thinking. My object in this book has been to explain what it is like to read Plutarch, and what I think one needs to bear in mind in order to read him with understanding. I have tried to do this in a manner intelligible to those who do not read Greek, though naturally I hope that what I have to say may be useful also to those who do. I have been generous with quotations, because it seems to me that to confront the prospective reader with particular texts and analyses of them is probably the best way of furnishing him with the clues he will need. The translations are my own; one important element in Plutarch's writing, the dignified movement of his flexible and comprehensive periods, evaporates in modern English, and I have made little attempt to preserve it.

There has been a great deal of scholarly work on Plutarch in recent years, especially in France. My debt to this, and to many older works, will be obvious. The very selective bibliography in the notes and Appendix will, I hope, suffice to give readers with various needs a reasonable indication of where to turn next.

A word on references. Those of the form '333C' are to the *Moralia*; they give the conventional page numbers, and the treatise concerned can be readily identified from the list in the Appendix. Where there is a general reference to a whole treatise, this normally takes the form of the number of the page on which it begins. The *Lives* are, as is customary, referred to by title and chapter; the Fragments by Sandbach's numbers.

It is a particular pleasure to acknowledge the constant encouragement and help of the General Editor of the series.

CHAPTER ONE

Plutarch[1]

CHAERONEA, Plutarch's birthplace, was a small town. One reason why he stayed at home was 'to prevent it from getting smaller'. Yet it was a historic place. Legend located there the death and burial of a party of Amazons, history recorded Philip's defeat of the Greek cities in 338 B.C. and Sulla's of Mithridates in 86 B.C.[2] Plutarch breathed history, and not only the splendour of it but the misery. For the Mithridatic war and the civil wars that followed had left devastation behind, here as in the rest of Greece. There were bitter memories, especially of Antony's war:

My great-grandfather Nicarchus used to tell how all the citizens were forced to carry a certain quantity of corn to the sea at Anticyra, with a whip at their backs to lend encouragement. They had taken one consignment, another had been measured out, and they were about to set forth again, when the news arrived of Antony's defeat. The city was saved! (*Antony* 58)

Whatever the causes, the depopulation of the most famous centres of mainland Greece was a notorious enough fact by the first century B.C. to be a commonplace *exemplum* of the mutability of human affairs:

Aegina lay behind me, Megara in front, Piraeus to the right, Corinth to the left. Once flourishing cities, now they lie prostrate and in ruins before our eyes. I thought to myself: 'Ah me, are we mere humans angry if someone dies . . . when the corpses of all these cities lie cast upon the ground together?'[3]

[1] On the subject of the whole chapter, see especially C. P. Jones, *Plutarch and Rome*, 1–66.

[2] *Demosthenes* 2, *Theseus* 27, *Demosthenes* 19, *Sulla* 15 ff.

[3] Servius Sulpicius in a consolatory letter to Cicero: Cic. *Ad fam.* 4.5.4.

The whole country, Plutarch makes one of his characters say, 'could hardly put three thousand hoplites in the field, the number Megara alone sent to Plataea' (413F). No wonder the oracles were deserted. Boeotia especially seemed a place of the past. Thebes had shrunk to its citadel hill; weeds enveloped statues in the agora.[4]

But the complaints, appropriate to the time of Cicero and Augustus, were becoming fainter and less real. It is an important feature of Plutarch's world, decisive perhaps in forming the optimism that is characteristic of him, the temper that could admire the past without despairing of the present, that he witnessed a revival in his own country, not yet the full-blown ostentation of the Greek world under the Antonines, but a promise and a sense of things stirring.

He would be about twenty when Nero visited Greece. The visit lasted from the summer of A.D. 66 to early 68. Roman writers find it hard to take seriously the emperor's aesthetic interests, the rhodomontade of the Proclamation of Liberty, and the abortive attempt at a Corinth Canal. But to the Greeks it was real and important. A generation later, Plutarch was writing one of his imitations of the Platonic underworld myths. The visionary Thespesius sees the souls of the wicked:

Among these appeared the soul of Nero, already in evil plight, pierced by red-hot nails. The workmen had prepared for it the form of a viper, as described by Pindar,[5] in which it was to be conceived and come to life by eating its way through its mother. But at this moment a great light suddenly shone forth, and a voice spoke from out of the light, bidding them change him into a gentler species, fashioning a singing creature of marsh and pool; for he paid the penalty for his crimes, and moreover the gods owed him a favour, because he had liberated Greece, the best and most god-favoured nation among his subjects. (567E)

In a myth one can say more than in plain speech. The bizarre fantasy in which the matricidal emperor is re-born as a frog

---

[4] Dio Chrysostom 7.121.

[5] Or perhaps 'Nicander'; see *Theriaca* 128 ff., and J. Dumortier in *Actes du VIIIᵉ Congrès de l'Association Budé*, Paris 1969, 552 ff.

enables Plutarch to combine without offence two points of view: Nero was a monster, as everyone agreed; at the same time he was the liberator, and the revival of Greek aspirations could be dated to the stimulus and incentive of his visit. For it is from this time onwards that we begin to see the efflorescence of that strange form of public life, composed of art, literature and festival, which the wealthier Greeks of the second century developed, and whose monuments, in word and stone, are among the most grandiose and impressive that survive from antiquity.[6] Plutarch's work belongs to the earlier and saner phase of this renascence.

Nero's visit to Delphi forms the background to another of Plutarch's 'Pythian dialogues', written a generation or more later. Here he represents himself, an enthusiastic student, discussing theological problems with his Platonist teacher, the Athenian Ammonius, and a group of friends (385B). It is an older man's nostalgic picture; the setting must be assumed fictitious, the autobiographical detail stylised and selective. But the choice of occasion remains significant; this was an epoch for Plutarch and his generation.

But we do not know much of the young Plutarch. There are no works that can be shown to have been written in youth, though there are a few rhetorical trifles which it is charitable to think of as youthful. Such are *Do Not Borrow* (827D), *Ills of the Body and Ills of the Mind* (500B), *Love of Offspring* (493A). Most of what we have, indeed most of what he wrote, is of middle age or later. There is indeed often a tone of intimacy and self-revelation in his writing;[7] but hardly anything is datable, and there seems little hope of tracing any significant development of style or thought.[8]

Family facts are few. They were well-to-do people, and had

[6] Among recent works on the 'second sophistic', which is only marginally important for Plutarch, see especially: G. W. Bowersock, *Greek Sophists in the Roman Empire*, Oxford 1969; E. L. Bowie, 'The Greeks and their Past', *Past and Present* 46 (1970) 3–41; and, for the literature, B. P. Reardon, *Courants littéraires grecs des IIe et IIIe siècles . . .*, Paris 1971.

[7] This was noted in antiquity: Eunapius, *Lives of the Philosophers*, p. 346, Wright.

[8] C. P. Jones, *JRS* 56 (1966) 61–74; H. G. Ingenkamp, *Plutarchs Schriften über die Heilung der Seele*, 1971. Jones goes as far as one reasonably can; Ingenkamp is very cautious.

roots in the history of that part of Greece. Plutarch's half-brother Timon claimed descent from the Opheltadai and from Daiphantus, historic Boeotian and Phocian names (558A). There cannot have been many families as wealthy and cultivated in and around Chaeronea, but it is evident from the long roll of local friends whom Plutarch mentions that he did not lack for agreeable and educated companionship. Grandfather Lamprias, 'at his most inventive and eloquent in his cups' (622F), is always remembered with pleasure. So is Plutarch's father, probably named Autobulus, a congenial figure who always kept good horses (642A)—fair proof of considerable means—and evidently stimulated his sons' intellectual and public activities. We cannot even guess the name of Plutarch's mother. Of his brothers, Lamprias is most often mentioned, a shrewd, bluff, humorous fellow, often appearing in dialogue-scenes (617E, 726D, 740A) and sometimes given a major part to play, as in *The Decline of Oracles* and *The Face in the Moon*. Timon too is spoken of in terms of close affection (487D). It is plain that the family as a group played a part in the social and intellectual life which Plutarch sought to immortalise in his writings. They also possessed political influence; they were among the natural local leaders, the sort of people who might be sent on embassies to proconsuls. Young Plutarch himself went on one, and tells an improving story about it. His colleague got left behind, and he had to transact the business himself. 'Always report in the plural' advised his father on his return; 'say "we", not "I" ' (816D).

It was naturally to Athens that Plutarch went to study philosophy. The tradition of the schools there had been virtually continuous since the time of Plato: it was to persist for another four or five centuries. The city became a second home; in the end he acquired citizen-rights there, and Athenian families later claimed descent from him. His was to be a life of learning, historical as well as philosophical: Athens offered what Chaeronea never could, abundance of books and a living tradition of continuity with the past. One could know a descendant of Themistocles.[9]

⁹ *Themistocles* 32.

One might, Plutarch observes, be a good man anywhere; to be a learned one requires these further aids.[10] His teacher in philosophy was the Platonist Ammonius, one of the great Athenians of the day, not only distinguished in his own line, but three times *stratēgos*, holding an office which gave him much general management of urban affairs, as well as powers over the study and discipline of students.[11] In Book Nine of *Table Talk*, Plutarch later published a group of short dialogues, set at Athens, the dramatic date of which seems to be in the seventies, in which he introduces a number of characters not to be found in the better-known circle of his later friends. Presumably this is a memorial to student days. From this and from other later writings there emerges a picture of the young Plutarch as he subsequently wished to appear. We see him a passionate student of mathematics (388F), interested too in all sorts of religious and philosophical matters.

We hear something also of his marriage and family, though it is surprisingly difficult to make a coherent story. His wife's father was called Alexion, and was probably from Chaeronea; the lady's own name seems to have been Timoxena. In *A Book of Love* (749B), Plutarch, writing towards the end of his life, makes his own son Autobulus recall a distant conversation, which took place shortly after his father and mother married. There was apparently some dispute among the bride's relations—whether or not about the marriage is not clear. She was brought by her husband, the young Plutarch, to the festival of Eros at Thespiae—then the most considerable town in Boeotia—to sacrifice and to make, or pay, a vow. Many family friends were there. In his dialogue, Plutarch uses this great occasion in his own life to provide a setting for a romantic story about a young man and an older lady of Thespiae and also for a philosophical discussion on different kinds of love. There were, anyway, sons of the marriage, probably four, and one daughter, Timoxena, who died in infancy, the subject of the moving and justly admired *Consolation to My Wife* (608A). It is perhaps a testimony to the quality of

[10] *Demosthenes* 2.
[11] C. P. Jones, 'The Teacher of Plutarch', *HSCP* 71 (1966) 205–13.

family life in Plutarch's circle that he stands out among ancient
moralists for his sympathetic and congenial attitudes to marriage
and children.[12] And we may notice another thing: the way in
which the women of this group were apparently expected to have
a good deal of literary and philosophical culture, which was seen
as a prophylactic against the feminine sins of frivolity and superstition. The *Consolation* assumes this; it contrives to be both a
moving document of personal feeling and a skilful adaptation of
the literary *topoi* of comfort, handled allusively and with sophistication. It seems likely that Plutarch's wife herself wrote a book:
To Aristylla, On Personal Adornment.[13] Clea, the daughter of the
friends for whose wedding Plutarch wrote *Advice on Marriage*,
grew up, it seems, to be a priestess at Delphi and the addressee of
two learned treatises: *Isis and Osiris* and *Brave Deeds of Women*.

The family grew and prospered. We hear of various younger
connections by marriage, presumably nieces' husbands. But the
prosperity did not lead to the dangerous world of politics.
Plutarch's descendants in the next two centuries prided themselves
rather on belonging to an academic dynasty. His nephew Sextus
appears as a teacher of Marcus Aurelius;[14] Lucius, the hero of
Apuleius' novel, claims descent from this side of Plutarch's
family;[15] so does a later Nicagoras, known from an inscription.[16]
The line goes on into the fourth century.[17] Perhaps the preserva-
tion of so many of Plutarch's books is connected with this continuous family tradition, centred on the great educational capital
of Athens.

And perhaps all this served his fame better in the long run than
any instant success as a sophist. For that seems to have been
denied him. The hothouse of the 'second sophistic' was the
Asiatic mainland, especially Ephesus and Smyrna. It is fairly clear
that Plutarch had few contacts here. One short speech of flam-

---

[12] Lisette Goesler, *Plutarchs Gedanken über die Ehe*, Zürich 1962.
[13] 145A: a book on the same subject is listed in the 'Catalogue of Lamprias',
no. 113.
[14] M. Aurelius 1.9. But Sextus, unlike Plutarch, was a Stoic.
[15] Apuleius, *Metamorphoses* 1.1; P. G. Walsh, *The Roman Novel*, 182.
[16] Dittenberger, *Sylloge Inscriptionum Graecarum*[3] (= *SIG*[3]), 845.
[17] See below p. 144, on Himerius.

boyant moralising, comparing bodily and mental ills, seems to have been delivered in Asia, perhaps at Halicarnassus or Sardis (501E). From Sardis too came Menemachus, a rich young friend who had the benefit of *Advice on Public Life*, and probably also, when things went ill, of *Exile*. Two lost works[18] were addressed to, or directed against, Plutarch's greatest literary contemporary, Dion of Prusa. One of these is said to have been spoken at Olympia—an appearance in the grandiose world of the great festivals. If we had these books, we might modify our impression that Plutarch was only on the fringe of the growing world of successful orators and sophists. As it is, it is difficult to get rid of the suspicion that he tried to break in and failed,[19] and that his epidictic style was as uncongenial to contemporaries as it seems packed and overloaded to us. His talents lay elsewhere, and they were more enduring.

He did however travel a good deal. He visited Alexandria, and he shows much interest in Egyptian things, most significantly in his great work on the myth of Isis and Osiris. More important, he went to Rome at least twice, and travelled in Italy, with some public business and not only as a philosophical lecturer. On one occasion, he relates (522D), he was giving a lecture to an audience which included Arulenus Rusticus, 'whom Domitian afterwards killed through envy of his reputation'. A soldier arrived with 'a letter from Caesar'. The class was silent, Plutarch paused. But Rusticus put the letter aside unopened: a perfect example of freedom from the vice of curiosity (*polupragmosunē*). It is usually supposed that this happened in Domitian's reign and it is tempting to associate it with Rusticus' consulship (92). There is no proof of this; and the suggestion of the narrative, with 'Domitian' and 'Caesar' mentioned as though they were different, is perhaps for an earlier date, under Vespasian or Titus. It would not be surprising if Plutarch were lecturing in Rome in the seventies.

Another Italian episode was Plutarch's visit to the civil-war

[18] Nos. 204, 207 in the 'Catalogue of Lamprias'.

[19] E. R. Dodds, in his stimulating and charming 'Portrait of a Greek Gentleman', *Greece and Rome* 2 (1933) 97 ff., suggests rather that Plutarch chose to stay out of the race; this is probably too charitable.

battlefield of Betriacum in the company of L. Mestrius Florus, an Othonian by necessity (*Otho* 14) but later an intimate of Vespasian. This prominent consular had a particular connection with Plutarch: the *nomen* the family took when they received citizenship was Mestrius. Now the date of Mestrius' consulship is uncertain.[20] He was proconsul of Asia, probably in 82/3, but his connection with mainland Greece may well go back to the end of Nero's time. It may have been Plutarch's father who took the step to citizenship. The consequences were anyway important: influential friendships, equestrian status, and ultimately the great honour of *ornamenta consularia* and an honorific appointment as an imperial procurator in Achaea.[21] Most significantly, it made a Roman by adoption of the man whose most ambitious work was to be the *Parallel Lives*: a literary demonstration of the parity and partnership of Greece and Rome, each with its contribution to make towards the development of true political virtue. The intellectual unity of the Greco-Roman world was a precarious thing; Plutarch fitly represents it at the moment before the split became incurable.

Not that Plutarch had many illusions about the position of the Greek city-state. He warns his friend from Sardis:

You are both ruler and subject, in a city subordinate to proconsuls, to Caesar's procurators . . . See the senators' boots[22] above your head . . . On many has descended 'neck-chopper axe, dread punisher'—on your Pardalas and his friends, for instance, when they forgot the limitations of their position. (814D–F)

The aim of the Greek statesman could only be concord (824C). Of the other blessings of society, peace is assured by the ruling power, freedom is conceded up to a point, prosperity and population are the gifts of heaven. To all this Plutarch is resigned. He counsels against resistance.

[20] C. P. Jones, *Plutarch and Rome*, 49.
[21] ibid. 29–30.
[22] *Kaltioi, calcei*, symbolise the governor: Jones, op. cit., 133; J. J. Hartman, *De Avondzon des Heidendoms*, 194, also gets this right, though he emends the text needlessly.

He may not even have been very happy about the alternative to resistance, namely infiltration. It was a conspicuous feature of Flavian and Trajanic times that prominent Greeks co-operated in imperial rule and reached the senate and the highest magistracies. Plutarch in one passage draws a disturbing lesson (470c). It destroys peace of mind to be too ambitious, not to be content with power in Bithynia or Galatia, but to want Roman status, the praetorship, then the consulship, then to be elected first on the list . . . This may not be a specific objection to the aspirations of Greeks for Roman magistracies. It seems unlikely that the addressee, Paccius, is of Greek origin. The whole development may well be on a universal moral plane, with no special pointedness in the example.[23] But it reads as though there were some sting in it, and it would certainly fit in with Plutarch's general attitudes to suppose that he is here preaching modesty to the Greek partners of empire, as he preaches humanity to the Roman.

It is Plutarch's ordinary practice to dedicate what he writes to a friend or prominent person. These dedications give us the clearest idea of the audience he sought. Some are to Greek notables, like the wealthy Spartan Herculanus or the Athenian Euphanes. Others are to literary men like Dion of Prusa or the Stoic Serapion, a piece of whose clumsy poem on medical ethics has been preserved on stone.[24] But many are to people of obvious political influence on the level of imperial administration: Terentius Priscus, the recipient also of Book XII of Martial's epigrams, or else his son; L. Herennius Saturninus, proconsul of Achaea in 97/8 or 98/9; T. Avidius Quietus and C. Avidius Nigrinus, brothers who in their turn were governors of Achaea and whose sons followed similar careers.[25] The Avidii lead us towards the

[23] The parallel with Seneca *De Ira* 3.31.2 has been thought to imply that the Roman colouring is from Panaetius. This does not follow. And the special feature of our passage is the succession by which local Asiatic influence leads to Roman magistracies. This reflects Plutarch's age, not Panaetius'.

[24] J. H. Oliver, *Hesperia*, Supplement viii (1949), 243.

[25] Jones (op. cit., 51 ff.) suggests that *Brotherly Love*, dedicated to the two elder Avidii, was written in the early nineties. But there is no proof that Nigrinus died then; he is simply not heard of later. The treatise has points in common with other treatises, and with the *Lives*. It suggests that one of the brothers is a great

circle of Pliny's correspondents, as also does C. Minicius Fundanus, consul in 107, with whose entourage Plutarch claims to be
on familiar terms. Most impressive of all is the great Q.
Sosius Senecio (consul 99 and 107) to whom the *Parallel Lives* were
dedicated; one of the great men of Trajan's reign, perhaps himself of Greek origin,[26] and apparently an intimate of Plutarch's of
long standing. It looks as if Plutarch too regarded the new order
that followed the death of Domitian as sunshine after storm.

The impressive list prompts two reflections. It is probably a
mistake to think of it all as an assault on the centres of influence
by the weapon of old acquaintance, with the *ornamenta* and the
procuratorship as belated tangible rewards. Plutarch was not
much, if at all, in Rome under Trajan. His life was centred now
on Chaeronea and Delphi. He was nobody's *éminence grise*, and
it is the merest speculation to try to fit him into patterns of influence and patronage of which we happen to have some historical
knowledge. Pliny does not mention him; it remains an open
question whether this is due to ignorance or to deliberate omission. Tacitus[27] might just have him in mind when he snipes at
Greeks who admire only their own history. Plutarch, any reader
may legitimately suspect, was not a successful orator; there is no
reason to think that any other substantial political success came
his way.[28]

Secondly: these complimentary dedications do not necessarily
prove the degree of intimacy which they superficially imply. They
are of course a familiar feature of ancient literature. And it is
natural to ask what the facts of the situation really were, in what
tone of friendship or dependence the real people talked. This is

---

man, while the other (Nigrinus) chose a quiet life (486D). It refers also to nephews
who are doing well. All the conditions are met by a date under Nerva or Trajan,
the period of Plutarch's greatest literary activity.

[26] C. P. Jones, *JRS* 60 (1970) 103.

[27] *Annals* 2.88: Graecorum ... qui sua tantum mirantur. But not only would
this be unfair, the context does not support a specific allusion: Greeks and
Romans are alike neglectful of the barbarian greatness of Arminius—the Greeks
out of patriotic vanity, the Romans out of regard for the past and disparagement
of the present.

[28] For a different emphasis, see Jones' book in general; also G. W. Bowersock,
Greek Sophists in the Roman Empire, 110 ff.

particularly so when the book or the poem is about manners or personal relationships, or when it is tempting to believe that there is some special point or even barb in the address. For example, Horace[29] praises the integrity of the rather disreputable Lollius; readers have sought irony in the poem. Plutarch makes Minicius Fundanus, who obviously had a reputation for bad temper, take pride in the cure of his irascibility; it seems a damaging revelation of a public man's failings. But if we look at the core of the matter, it is inconceivable that either Horace or Plutarch should be making a covert attack. The dedication is a compliment; that is the fundamental rule. Nothing associated with it can therefore be meant to cause offence. *Control of Anger* (452E) is about one of the most commonly discussed moral failings of the age. Fundanus is complimented just by having such a useful and elegant book addressed to him, and piquancy is added to the compliment by representing him as a successful self-improver. Besides, irascibility (like gout) is to some extent a disease of power and wealth; only important people need this sort of advice, and so it is flattering to be offered it.

Now there also appear in Plutarch, sometimes as addressees, more often as characters in dialogues, a host of humbler persons, a hundred or more: family, neighbours in the small Boeotian and Phocian towns, fellow-students, a dozen or so doctors, teachers of literature, philosophers. The same principle generally applies: when they are mentioned, they are complimented. A clear example is young Diogenianus in *The Pythia's Prophecies* (395A), enthusiastic and courteous, worthy son of a good father. Some of the multitude come to life through Plutarch's not unskilful character drawing. Some are known from inscriptions or other sources. Philinus of Chaeronea, a vegetarian and a fellow-traveller on a journey to Rome, set up a bust of Plutarch 'his benefactor', years afterwards, when Plutarch was dead.[30] Also from Chaeronea were Soclarus, who bore the *nomen* Mestrius, like Plutarch himself, and the Niger who came to an unfortunate end:

---

[29] *Odes* 4.9.
[30] 660D: *SIG*³ 843B.

When he was practising as a sophist (*sophisteuōn*) in Galatia,[31] he swallowed a fishbone. Another outside sophist appeared and gave a speech, and Niger, afraid to give the impression of defeat, spoke himself, with the bone still stuck in his throat. Severe and obstinate inflammation set in, and, unable to bear the pain, he submitted to a deep cut from outside. The bone was removed through the wound, but the wound itself festered and became infected, and it killed him. (131A)

'As a sophist': this is a word Plutarch never uses of himself, but generally treats as pejorative, much as Plato had done. Used of Niger, it implies that Plutarch does not much approve of his compatriot's career. He did indeed write a book against the sophists—apparently a piece of literary history, attacking the style of Gorgias and its influence.[32]

In *The Decline of Oracles* (410A), learned men come to Delphi from the ends of the earth: Cleombrotus the Spartan had returned from philosophical travels in Egypt, Ethiopia and the East; Demetrius, the grammarian of Tarsus, was on his way home from Britain. Both are people of some significance: Cleombrotus for his bizarre learning and theological speculations, Demetrius because he is almost certainly to be identified with the Demetrius who made dedications at York to Ocean and Tethys and to the gods of the imperial praetorium.[33]

Apart from visits to Athens and other places in northern Greece, like the health-resort of Aedepsus in Euboea, with its comforts and cultivated spa-society (667C), Plutarch seems to have spent most of his later life in Chaeronea or in Delphi. He was a citizen of both. It was probably at Delphi that he died, in the early years of Hadrian but before 125, shortly after dreaming (or so we are told) of ascending into heaven under the guidance of Hermes.[34] The two communities joined in honouring him with a bust and

[31] This could mean Gaul, where Greek sophistic activity did exist (a younger contemporary, the great Favorinus, came from Arles); but it seems slightly more likely that it should be the Asiatic province.

[32] Fr. 186, 192 Sandbach. Hence the various attitudes of later sophists and philosophers to Plutarch: below, p. 144.

[33] *Roman Inscriptions of Britain*, 662–3; see R. M. Ogilvie—I. A. Richmond, *Tacitus: Agricola*, 32 ff.

[34] Artemidorus 4.72.

an epitaph that tastelessly echoes Simonides' lines on the dead of
Thermopylae:

> Delphians and Chaeroneans erected this statue together,
> obeying the ordinance of the Amphictyons.[35]

His activity in both places is central to the understanding of his
literary work, most of which was produced here, in the happy days
of Nerva and Trajan.

The household at Chaeronea became a kind of philosophical
school, nothing very formal perhaps, but a place where young
people from a wide area of Greece could pursue philosophy and
rhetoric. The dialogue *The Intelligence of Animals* (959A) presents, doubtless in an idealised form, the life of the centre and its
'family atmosphere'—if one may use so anachronistic a phrase.
Autobulus, whom we take to be Plutarch's father, is discovered
talking to Soclarus. They are discussing an encomium on hunting
given the day before by someone unnamed, perhaps intended to
be Plutarch himself—anyway, someone who had let his rhetoric
rust but has revived it to keep in with the young men. Autobulus,
though moved by the encomium, has reservations. He fears that
cruelty to animals may lead to cruelty to men—an attitude that
he attributes to the Pythagoreans, though it is also characteristic
of Plutarch himself and fits in with the theory of moral *askēsis*
(exercise) which he develops in various contexts.[36] Autobulus
goes on:

> Yesterday, as you know, we propounded the theory that all animals
> have *some* share in intellect and reason. We then proposed the topic of
> the comparative intelligence of creatures of sea and land, as an agreeable
> and educational debating subject for our young men. We shall be
> judging the debate today, I fancy, if Aristotimus and Phaedimus and
> their friends take up the challenge. (960A)

They do. When Soclarus and Aristobulus have had a preliminary
discussion on animal intelligence, the young men appear, replete
with examples from sea and land, to make the case on either side.

---

[35] *SIG*³ 843A.
[36] See Chapter 5. On kindness to animals, note especially *Cato the Elder* 5.

One spokesman is Aristotimus, a young man from Delphi. His supporters include his own brother, another relative of Autobulus, and one Nicander. The other party, under Phaedimus, includes Heracleon of Megara and Philostratus of Euboea. These are appropriately enough the sea-folk. Optatus, a contemporary of Autobulus, acts as judge. His Roman name is worth noting; it does not of course mean that he was not as Greek as the others. It is natural, and no doubt correct, to suppose that all these are real people, pupils and friends from nearby parts of Greece, who would be gratified to see their names in the book.

If we try to define the date of the dialogue and be more specific about it historically, we encounter difficulties. But we may perhaps believe in a dramatic date in the eighties. If the rhetorical encomiast on hunting is Plutarch, it is a Plutarch of mature years, though his father is alive and active. Aristotimus says (974A) that he was present at a show by a performing dog in the theatre of Marcellus in Rome when 'the old man Vespasian' was also there. This seems to imply a dramatic date after Vespasian's death; we may think it unlikely that this young man had in fact been in Rome, but the chronology seems consistent and possible. The conventions of dialogue allow anachronisms and vagueness; but there is enough realism in this to make us feel we have a consistent picture of what Plutarch wanted his school to look like.

Plutarch also had a public life, and to some extent his statements about this can be controlled. It was the life of a wealthy man, a natural leader in his own community. Chaeronea brought its local public duties, in which even humble office gave him satisfaction. With proud modesty he compares himself to Epaminondas, who consented to be a *telearchos*, an official concerned with street-cleaning and the disposal of dirt and drainage. Evidently visitors found it amusing to see the learned teacher occupied in the humbler kind of supervision of municipal works (811B). Delphi offered wider scope.

The ancient oracle, 'the navel of the world', was making a bid for revival as a great festival centre. The Roman administration helped. Augustus' devotion to Apollo led him to favour Delphi, and associate his new city of Nicopolis with the Amphictyony. Later emperors continued support. Domitian restored the temple burnt down in 84, a proconsul advised (or gave instructions) on the arrangements for the Pythian festival in 90.[37] There is a good deal of inscriptional evidence for new building towards the end of the century, and names familiar from Plutarch appear:[38] Flavius Soclarus, *epimelētēs* ('administrator') when a library and a new house for the prophetess was constructed; Petraeus, twice *agōnothĕtēs* ('marshal of the games'), the generous donor of a statue of Trajan; finally 'Mestrius Plutarchus' the priest, *epimelētēs* when a statue to Hadrian was erected. Plutarch was then an old man; when a further statue of the emperor was required in 125, someone else is found in charge. His 'many Pythiads' of service were over.

The Pythia's Prophecies (394D ff.) gives the most vivid picture of Plutarch's Delphi. Young Diogenianus is escorted by friends and professional guides (*periēgētai*)—an unscholarly class, apparently, of whom the serious investigator thinks very little—up the Sacred Way to the temple of Apollo, past various treasures and monuments that require explanation. The main subject of the conversation is, naturally enough, divination, one of Plutarch's favourite topics. The principal speaker is called Theon; he seems very much the author's spokesman. After a long discussion, Theon comes to speak of the present state of affairs. All is peace and tranquillity; no revolutions, tyrannies or plagues. So no need to ask the oracle anything but everyday questions: 'Ought I to marry?' 'Ought I to travel?' 'Ought I to lend money?' It would be ostentatious to dress up the answers to such inquiries in poetry. We should be content with plain prose, and not wonder anxiously why oracles are no longer given in hexameters. Anyone would think we were afraid that the place might lose its thousand years' reputation. It is anyway inconsistent to admire the concise wisdom of the Delphic maxims 'Know thyself' and 'Nothing too much', and then complain that the oracles are expressed in simple

[37] *SIG*³ 821D. [38] e.g. *SIG*³ 823, 829.

language. The prophetess' plain words

have filled the oracle with dedications and gifts from foreigners and Greeks and adorned it with the beautiful buildings and constructions of the Amphictyony . . . Pylaea[39] flourishes and grows as Delphi does, acquiring a grace and beauty and splendour of temples, halls and fountains, such as she never had these thousand years . . . I love myself for being eager and serviceable for these duties, with Polycrates[40] and Petraeus; I love also our leader (*kathēgĕmōn*) in this policy, the deviser and planner of most of these advances. (408F–409C)

This is not easy to interpret. If we assume that Theon is a distinct character, whether real or, as some have thought, fictitious, and anyway not a mere cover-name for Plutarch, it is proper to assume that in so obviously personal a passage he is speaking as Theon, in other words that *he* is the zealous associate of Petraeus and Polycrates. Who then is the *kathegemon*? It cannot be Apollo, because the passage goes on to contrast divine aid with human, and this sentence must be referring to human activity. It has often been thought a loyal tribute to Hadrian; and this is perfectly possible, especially as the emperor seems to have been given the archonship at Delphi in the first years of his reign. A third possibility is that it is Plutarch himself. The obvious objection is the apparent immodesty; but we may compare the beginning of Cicero's *De Legibus*, where Quintus Cicero is made to declare that his brother's poetry is immortal. Nor would it be an unjustified boast. Plutarch's thought and care for Delphi extended over many years. His knowledge of its traditions and antiquities was vast. He will have been involved in all its controversies and plans. We hear of a few episodes: debates over the content of the competitions (674E), the advocacy of a claim by the Lykormai and Satilaioi to ancient privileges accorded the descendants of Heracles (558B). These will be samples of a lifetime of service.

Delphi, then, was the main sphere of Plutarch's practical achievement. Concern for these local and, as it were, ecclesiastical matters formed the background to his life as a writer. But what he did for the new buildings of Delphi was nothing to the liter-

[39] i.e. the sister shrine of Demeter at Thermopylae.   [40] cf. 667E, *Aratus* 1.

ary monument he was building for himself, the vast *oeuvre* whose surviving half fills twenty-six Loeb volumes and has, more significantly perhaps than the work of any other single writer, educated Europe in the central historical and moral traditions of classical antiquity. His life offers a clue to the nature of his writing; for it also was devoted to the restoration and interpretation of a tradition. Plutarch's aim was to convey the essence of Hellenic *paideia* to his pupils, to his powerful contemporaries, and to posterity. With posterity, at least, he succeeded beyond all hope.

CHAPTER TWO

Language, Style and Form

THERE are extant forty-eight Lives by Plutarch, all but four of which belong to the series of Greek and Roman 'parallels'. There are also over seventy short works of miscellaneous content. These are commonly called *Moralia*, a translation of the Greek *ēthika*, a title used in the Middle Ages for one considerable group of them concerned with topics in practical ethics. The corpus as we have it is in fact the result of various mediaeval Byzantine efforts at collecting books by Plutarch, culminating in the magnificent manuscripts written under the direction of Maximus Planudes at the end of the thirteenth and the beginning of the fourteenth century.[1] It contains a number of works which are certainly spurious, though some of them are historically of great value and interest; *The Education of Children, Fate, Doctrines of the Philosophers, Lives of the Ten Orators, On Music*, are all books which we are fortunate to possess. For our knowledge of what was not harvested in the mediaeval collections we depend largely on quotations in later writers like the fourth-century Christian compiler Eusebius and the fifth-century anthologist Stobaeus. There is however another source of information on the titles of lost works, a catalogue supposed to have been compiled by a son of Plutarch called Lamprias.[2] There is no other evidence that there ever was any such person, and the list apparently dates from late antiquity, perhaps the fourth century, when Plutarch was much read. It comprises 227 titles, including a number of Lives now lost, and

---

[1] See below, p. 147.
[2] Conveniently edited and translated by F. H. Sandbach, Loeb *Moralia*, vol. xv.

some 130 other lost works. Its arrangement seems haphazard: the Lives come first, then the longer works, then those in single books, but with very little principle of grouping. It omits some genuine books that survive; on the other hand it includes some extant *spuria*, so that we must conclude that some of the unknowns may be spurious also. It includes in fact (no. 56) Aristotle's *Topics*, which no one in his right mind can have thought Plutarch's.

Now the attribution of books in antiquity was a chancy business. Galen[3] gives a curious account of the fortunes of his own works. He would sometimes give copies to friends, with no name on the title, without intending them to go into circulation. When the owners died, the books fell into the hands of the heirs and came to be regarded as the owners' own compositions. The true authorship being discovered, the copies would come back to Galen for correction. Thus in the conditions of book circulation that prevailed in Plutarch's time and later, it could easily have happened that the contents of a collection of books that had belonged to him or was in the family could be thought to be all his work.

But however much we pare down the list, it remains formidable: some two hundred and fifty *biblia*. Many later Greeks however, especially philosophers, wrote on this scale; what is unusual with Plutarch is the survival of such a high proportion. The causes of this invite conjecture; the popularity of Plutarch in the Christian Greek world from the fourth century onwards must have been an important factor.

Galen observes in the same context that anyone who was properly trained not only in medicine and philosophy but in *grammatikē* would know within a few lines if a book was not by him. The trouble was that many would-be philosophers were unable to read properly and had never had a real grammatical training. This is testimony that, even at this late period, individual tricks of Greek style were recognisable by the expert. If we could resurrect a suitably educated second-century Greek, we should no

[3] *On His Own Books*, xix, 8 Kühn.

doubt find the same with Plutarch. Indeed, we should not be too diffident about our own senses in this department; disputes about the authorship of works in the corpus do exist, and rightly so, but the obvious homogeneity of Plutarch's characteristic style and presentation have made them few and not too serious. It is no accident that the most doubtful points concern the collections of *apophthegmata*, which have not been 'worked up' stylistically.

The style indeed is very much 'the man himself'. Plutarch forged and thoroughly controlled a remarkably facile and rich linguistic instrument. Learned and allusive, imaginative and metaphorical, exuberant and abundant, his writing also has qualities which are the reverse of its virtues: it is unequal, uneconomical, a good deal removed from the simplicity we associate—though not always justly—with classical Attic. But it is a mode of expression exactly tuned to his attitudes to the world; in its way, it is a great achievement, and it had very wide and persistent influence on later writers, Christian as well as pagan, modern as well as ancient.

Plutarch and his contemporaries faced a language problem. It is a feature of Greek, as of much Latin, literature that its language diverges widely from that of the author's daily speech. Greek poetry, from its earliest phases, was a linguistic evocation of the archaic or the exotic. By Hellenistic times, poetry could only be written in studied reproductions of archaic dialects. To a less extent, the same is true of prose. Here, the classical age, the fourth century B.C., did indeed develop an Attic style which, mainly because of the importance of forensic oratory, was essentially the vernacular. The history of prose is thereafter one of successive reforms and revivals, aimed generally at maintaining this fourth-century Attic. The greater and more rapid the changes in living speech, the more radical the periodical reform had to be. One such reform, an important one, took place two generations before Plutarch, and is documented in the theory and practice of Dionysius of Halicarnassus, who lived for many years at Rome under Augustus. Dionysius rejected all post-Attic prose as bizarre, eccentric or disorganised; his remedy was a better use of the resources of the Attic classics, and especially the orators. This was archaism, but a positive and constructive archaism, which sought to enrich rather than restrict by prescribing models to imitate. It is quite distinct from the later archaism of the second-century Atticists, who compiled lists of words authorised by classical usage, and tried to confine themselves within these limits. Dionysius' work on word-arrangement (*sunthesis onomatōn*) makes it particularly clear what his essential aims were: he wanted to exploit the versatility and vigour he found in the classics, so as to accommodate the intellectual excitement of pathos and rhetoric, which sophisticated readers now needed, in a disciplined but varied prose.

Plutarch inherited a situation in which this classicising revolution was an important factor. Not that he thought much of Dionysius himself. When he comes to use him as a historical source, in the lives of the early Roman heroes and especially in *Coriolanus*, he imitates him little and improves on him a good deal.[4] Dionysius' friend Caecilius of Caleacte, the opponent answered by the author of *On the Sublime*, is also no favourite of Plutarch's, who thinks of him as pedantic and pretentious—'a dolphin on dry land' for trying to judge Cicero's style.[5] Plutarch is of course by profession a philosopher, and it is therefore traditional for him to make fun of the rhetoricians and their juggling with words.[6]

But he is himself a conscious artist in an elaborate manner, meticulous in his periodic structures, his studied word-patterns, his avoidance of hiatus, his carefully chosen vocabulary, and so on. This should not seem a paradox, either in Plutarch or, for example, in Seneca. Both worked in a tradition which demanded an extraordinarily high level of verbal expertise and sophistication; all they are saying, when they speak as philosophers, is that they claim to put sense first. Again, despite his coolness and silence about it, Plutarch is demonstrably, if unconsciously, a beneficiary of the changes instituted by the Greek Augustans: witness his varied syntax and sophisticated word-order. He writes

[4] I have discussed this relationship in *JRS* 53 (1963) 1 ff.
[5] *Demosthenes* 3.　　　　　[6] See below, pp. 31 ff.

what we may call a reformed Hellenistic Greek, with very few non-classical features of syntax[7] or morphology, enormously enriched by his vast reading. Dionysius himself had not restricted his vocabulary to words found in the Attic classics, but Plutarch is freer and more catholic altogether in his exploitation of the enrichments of style which come in after the close of the classical age. His vocabulary is three times that of Demosthenes, and much of it is poetical or post-Attic. He makes great use of the compound verbs in which Hellenistic Greek found both elegance and clumsiness. He fully shares the Hellenistic penchant for abstracts, even as subjects—in general an unclassical feature. An English schoolboy, asked to translate into Greek the sentence 'Kindness covers a wider area than justice' would probably be advised to try a paraphrase in more concrete terms: something like 'we treat more things kindly than we do justly'. By the usage of classical authors, this is fairly good advice. But the sentence as it stands is a literal translation of Plutarch (*Cato* 5) and typical enough of him. Sometimes the use of abstracts produces a concise effectiveness of which the language of earlier prose is hardly capable. 'Meanness tugs at the glutton's finger in the fish-market [i.e. stops him putting his finger up to indicate a bid]; avarice deflects lechery from an expensive whore' (706B).

The continuance of such features of Hellenistic writing marks Plutarch off from many of his contemporaries and most of his immediate successors, who went much further in their *mimēsis* of a narrow range of classics, and tended to reject whenever possible words which they could not find in the old writers. Plutarch is firmly enough set in the continuous tradition of Greek writing not to feel the need for this more radical classicism. His linguistic position indeed reflects his thought: the Greek past was alive for him, and its language a living instrument, through every phrase of which the past might be evoked and seen to be continuous with the present. If we think of a writer's language as the roof

---

[7] Obvious non-classical traits include *mē* for *ou* as the negative in most kinds of subordinate clause and participial phrase, and the very restricted, but in some ways unclassical, use of the optative.

to shelter his thoughts, Plutarch's was not a museum but an old and much-used house, still eminently fit to be lived in. Much of the flavour of course evaporates in translation. Plutarch's classic sixteenth-century translators,[8] Amyot and his disciples North and Holland, still best convey the richness and elaboration; but they do so at the cost of the control and elevation of tone which prevent the real Plutarch, however long-winded he is, from being garrulous. The weakness and strength of Amyot were correctly judged by Octave Gréard, in one of the most perceptive books on Plutarch ever written.[9] Plutarch's style, he says, 'ne revêt que par instants les formes de la naïveté, mais il en a l'âme. C'est cette âme dont Amyot s'est inspiré dans sa traduction.' More modern translations generally lose much of the brightness and vigour of the original. The translations in this book can be no exception. Modern English hardly seems to possess the stops that are necessary. The flavour of the loaded and allusive language, the rounded form of the periods, are discernible only in Greek; but the main rhetorical features of presentation, the *exempla* and imagery, the variety and abundance will perhaps shine dimly through.

Here to begin with is a typical passage of moral advice.

Such[10] is the contentment and change of heart that reasoning engenders in every life. When Alexander heard Anaxarchus discourse on the infinite number of worlds, he wept. When his friends asked what was wrong, he replied, 'Ought one not to weep, if there are infinite worlds and one is not yet master even of one?' But Crates, with his wallet and his cloak, spent his days in play and laughter as if life were one long holiday.

Agamemnon found it painful to have many subjects:

You will know the son of Atreus, Agamemnon,
whom Zeus thrusts always into trouble, above all other men.[11]

But Diogenes, when he was put up for sale, made fun of the auctioneer

---

[8] See below, pp. 150 ff.   [9] *La Morale de Plutarque*, 391.
[10] i.e. as sudden and complete as the change of attitude to food that comes with the passing of disease and the restoration of health.   [11] *Iliad* 10.85.

by lying down, and refused to get up when ordered, saying with a laugh, 'Suppose you were selling a fish . . .?'

Socrates had a philosophical conversation with his friends in prison. But Phaethon, when he went up to heaven, cried because no one would give him his father's horses and chariot.

So, as the shoe is shaped to the foot and not *vice versa*, attitudes assimilate lives to themselves. It is not true, as has been said, that habit makes the best life pleasant to those who choose it; in fact, wisdom makes one and the same life both best and pleasantest. Let us therefore purify the spring of contentment that is within us, so that external circumstances may for their part too deal with us as friends and familiars in return for our fair dealing:

> With circumstances one must not be angry;
> they cannot care. But if the encounterer
> handles them right, things will go well with him.[12]

For Plato compared life to a game of dice, in which one has to make the proper throw and use the throw advantageously. Now the throw itself is not in our control; but the appropriate acceptance of events from fortune and the allocation of them to areas in which what is welcome will do most good and what is unwanted least harm to those involved —all this *is* our concern, if we are wise. People who are unskilled and foolish about life are like invalids who cannot endure heat or cold. They are excited by good fortune, daunted by bad, and disturbed by both—or rather by themselves in both sets of circumstances, and not less in those that are supposed to be good. Theodorus the 'atheist' used to say that he offered his arguments with his right hand, but his audience took them with their left. Similarly, the untrained often take Fortune with the left hand, when she offers herself on the right, and so they make fools of themselves. The wise, on the other hand, often acquire something of service and value to themselves out of the most disagreeable events, just as bees derive honey from thyme, which is the driest and sharpest of herbs. (466D–467C)

This is a central passage in Plutarch's *Quiet of Mind*, 'a treatise,' as Philemon Holland says, 'where a man may see the excellent discourses and most sound arguments of moral philosophy'.[13]

---

[12] Euripides fr. 287 (from *Bellerophon*).
[13] Holland is in fact translating the *sommaire* added in many later editions of Amyot.

The subject—*euthumia, animi tranquillitas*—was one that had been much treated from the time of Democritus. The Stoic Panaetius 'made a particularly significant contribution to the tradition. Plutarch's book in fact is original only in selection and presentation. The passage we are considering makes a single, simple point: that a wise attitude to life produces contentment, whatever our circumstances. Everything else is supporting amplification: a text-book illustration of principles laid down by generations of rhetoricians for the use of examples (*paradeigmata*) and general thoughts (*enthumēmata, gnōmai*) to support a proposition.[14] First comes a series of *paradeigmata* in pairs: Alexander contrasted with Crates, Agamemnon with Diogenes, Socrates with Phaethon. In each pair, the difference between the contented and the discontented depends on the presence of reason; in each pair, the philosopher is seen to be the happier. The pairing could be Plutarch's own, except that Socrates and Phaethon appear again as a symbol of wisdom and folly in *Exile* (607F), and this suggests that this contrast at least is an inherited commonplace.

Two of the *exempla*, the stories of Anaxarchus and Diogenes, are in the form of anecdotes. In the terminology of the *rhetores*, they are *chreiai*. They relate wise and useful remarks by famous characters whose name guarantees the goodness of the lesson. Such anecdotes were gathered in collections even in classical times. Plutarch both used the collections of others and doubtless made his own—whether or not the extant sets of Spartan and other *apophthegmata* ('sayings') are his. The wording of such an anecdote was the free choice of the writer who wished to use it, provided of course that the main point was recognisable. Of these two stories, the one about Anaxarchus is in Valerius Maximus' huge collection, under the heading 'desire for glory'. His version concludes with an additional point: Alexander, though a man, was not satisfied with the dwelling that suffices for the gods.[15] The Diogenes story too occurs elsewhere. It is part of a cycle connected

[14] The essentials of the rhetorical doctrine are in Aristotle, *Rhetoric* 2.20–1.

[15] Val. Max. 8.14 ext. 2: compare 3.3 ext. 4. Valerius Maximus is one of the Latin authors whom Plutarch knew, though there is no likelihood of his having used him here.

with Diogenes' sale into slavery. In our other source, Diogenes Laertius, it is somewhat different:

Not being allowed to sit down, he said: 'It doesn't matter; fish are sold in any position.'[16]

This makes explicit the point which Plutarch's elegant aposiopesis leaves us to see for ourselves.

A second form of authoritative support is the poetical quotation. This device is as old as prose literature, or at least as old as Plato. Collections of suitable passages were made at an early period. In Menander's *Shield* (407 ff.), it is a comic detail for the clever slave to repeat to himself poetical saws (*gnōmai*) like

No man is happy in all things he does,

or

'Tis fortune makes man's world, and not good counsel.

These sayings often recur.[17] Besides the dramatists—inevitable in Menander, favourites also with the philosophers—Homer and Theognis are common sources. By Plutarch's time, collections and anthologies were legion. Plutarch will have both used and made such things, as he did with anecdotes; from this source, and also from his own reading, he held ready an enormous store of apt quotations, which do much to enhance the colour and variety of his writing, even if sometimes one can hardly restrain a smile at the appearance of an old favourite. For example, we shall probably never know what tragic poet wrote the line:

Plucking at heart-strings never plucked before.[18]

Nor can we know its original context: 'strings' (*chordai*) are mentioned once only in extant tragedy, and of a lyre. Our poet doubtless compared the heart to a stringed instrument; the image is banal in English. The line would be a godsend to a philosopher discussing the nature of the soul. Let us suppose that it is through some such intermediary that Plutarch knows it. He uses it in five

---

[16] Diogenes Laertius 6.27.
[17] The second one is in fact the 'text' of Plutarch's 'sermon' on fortune (97c).
[18] Tragica adespota 361 Nauck.

places: once of anger (456E), once comprehensively of anger, superstition, family quarrels and sex (43E), once of fever (501A) and once of drunkenness (657D); all these seem fairly natural applications of the idea. The fifth occurrence is more curious:

The portico at Olympia is called the Portico of Seven Voices because it produces many echoes from a single cry: and if the slightest word touches Garrulity, she immediately returns an echo,
Plucking at heart-strings never plucked before. (502D)

Here the quotation seems simply an intensifier, and perhaps gives a balance with the image that precedes. It is as though Plutarch this time could not think of anything more apt to fill out his sentence.

The lines from Euripides' *Bellerophon* in our passage from *Quiet of Mind* are not quite so familiar, but they are also an anthology piece. They recur in the great compilation of Stobaeus,[19] which gives us so much of the conventional lore of late antiquity, and Marcus Aurelius (7.38) thought it worth while copying part of the passage into the book of reflections he made for his own use and comfort.

It is not only as direct support that quotations and anecdotes are drawn in. When Plutarch writes in this passage

It is not true, as has been said, that habit makes the best life pleasant . . .

he is playing a trick which is of great importance in the texture of his writing. He has in mind a Pythagorean saying which he elsewhere approves:[20] the good life seems harsh at first, but habit makes even asceticism agreeable. To correct this forms a novel point; reflection on the original saying has stimulated a truer formulation. At the same time, it amounts to a device for introducing the quotation into an argument where it scarcely belongs. This is analogous to Plutarch's frequent use of an image not to point a similarity but to indicate a contrast; in a sense, this helps to make the picture more precise, but it easily turns into a device to cram something else into an already packed passage.

[19] iv. 350 and v. 968 Hense.   [20] See 123C, 602B.

One final point. Allusions apart, the passage, like most of Plutarch, contains a great deal of imagery. Much of this is conventional. The shoe,[21] the springs of contentment,[22] the throw of the dice,[23] the delicate invalid, the bees on the thyme,[24] are all symbols with a history of their own. It is typical of Plutarch that they should all be gathered together in such a short space; lavishness with imagery in any reflective or discursive context is one of the most distinctive characteristics of his prose. He seems always to be seeking implied or explicit comparisons between the subject in hand and something else. It all amounts, in a manner of speaking, to innumerable arguments from analogy. Like the authorities and the *exempla*, the imagery has a rhetorical function in support of the point being made. But it is far too rich and ubiquitous to have no other end. We should I think credit Plutarch with letting his imagery fulfil also a sort of poetic purpose. The neat comparison passes easily into a suggestive symbol, the arresting switch of theme into an imaginative vision.

Indeed, all the methods of support and amplification which this passage illustrates—anecdote, quotation, simile—have a depth and interest in Plutarch which is not easily explained in simple rhetorical terms. He is not really using this apparatus to convince so much as in a sort of imaginative play. He wants to remind the reader all the time of vast areas of philosophical and literary tradition, to provide a great deal of thematic variety, and to give the pleasure of surprise by the ingenuity with which familiar thoughts are turned in unfamiliar ways.

Quiet of Mind is a calm book, in form a letter. It is presented (464E) as a compilation of 'notes' (*hupomnēmata*) sent in response to a request. In it, the strident Cynic preaching is muted into grave reading-matter for the reflective Paccius. This quiet mode

[21] cf. Horace *Epist.* 1.7.98, 10.42; Aristippus fr. 67 Mannebach.
[22] cf. M. Aurelius 7.59.
[23] Plutarch wrote a book (Cat. Lampr. 105) on 'the likeness of life to a game of dice': cf. also Plato, *Republic* 604C; Sophocles fr. 947; [Plu.] *Consolation to Apollonius* 112E.
[24] e.g. 32A, 41F.

is not universal in Plutarch's moralising, though it is very common. We can detect other sorts of occasion and their corresponding styles, in which the same mechanism of allusion and imagery is used to achieve an overall effect of a distinctly different kind. Sometimes, the tradition of the real sermon, which scholars call the *diatribē*,[25] is nearer the surface. *Do Not Borrow!* is a case in point. It is a chaotic but vigorous address, presumably a public lecture. It has an unusual theme, and this has led to the conjecture that there was a topical point to it. 'Une plaie véritable, l'usure, dévorait Chéronée.'[26] Perhaps; but there can be no proof. The speech attracted attention among Plutarch's Christian imitators: St. Basil drew largely on it in his Homily on the Fourteenth Psalm. Packed with imagery, often obscure and confused in its transitions, it is one of those pieces that lend colour to the notion that Plutarch was at one time an over-ambitious and therefore unsuccessful speaker. There is naturally no proof that this little homily is early. What seems *iuvenilis ardor* may be just genre-colour. But it is a plausible guess.

This is how the piece ends (831B ff.):

Now I must turn to the richer and more delicate, the people who say 'Shall I then have no slaves, no hearth or home?' A man sick of the dropsy and swollen might as well say to his doctor 'Shall I then become thin and empty?' Why not, if it makes you healthy? It's the same with you. Have no slaves, so as to be no slave yourself. Have no property, so as not to be the property of another.

Listen to the fable about the vultures. One vulture was sick and said he was bringing up guts. 'What's wrong with that?' said the other vulture; 'they're not *your* guts, they're the corpse's we were tearing up just now.'

Debtors don't sell their own farms and houses, but farms and houses

---

[25] A useful term much used, since the publication of Usener's *Epicurea* (1887), to describe a lecture or discourse on a moral theme, marked by a combination of seriousness with humour and a certain vividness and immediacy in language. Typical examples in the remains of Teles (ed. O. Hense, 1909). The word is often used in discussions both of Roman Satire (N. Rudd, *The Satires of Horace*, ch. 1) and of moralists like Plutarch and Epictetus. Definition is difficult; but there is a distinct tradition which needs a name. The connotations of English *diatribe* confuse the issue. In Greek, *diatribe* is strictly 'way of passing time'. See J. L. Moles in *Oxford Classical Dictionary*, ed. 3, 463.

[26] O. Gréard, op. cit., 190.

belonging to the creditors they have made their masters according to the law.

'Yes, but my father left me this farm.' He also left you your freedom and your status, and you ought to think more about these. Your father made your foot and your hand for you, but if they rot, you pay the man who cuts them off.

Calypso dressed Odysseus 'in clothing sweetly-scented',[27] breathing flesh divine, a gift in memory of her love: but when he capsized and sank and surfaced with difficulty, the clothes were sodden and heavy, and he stripped and threw them off, and tied a scarf under his naked breast and 'swam along looking to landward'.[28] Once saved, he lacked neither for clothing nor for food. Well? Don't debtors face a storm, when the creditor at last appears and cries 'Hand over'?

'So speaking he gathered the clouds and ruffled the sea;
east wind and south and violent west fell on together',[29]

as debt rolls on top of debt. Swamped, the victim clings to the load that weighs him down, unable to swim to safety; down he goes, pushed to the bottom, sunk without trace, he and the friends who guaranteed him.

Crates the Theban, with no demand or debt upon him, disgusted with management and cares and distractions, abandoned a property worth eight talents, took his cloak and wallet, and fled for refuge to philosophy by way of poverty. Anaxagoras left his land to be grazed by sheep. But this is nothing to Philoxenus the lyricist, who had an allotment of land in a Sicilian colony, a good living and a household of considerable substance, but saw that luxury, soft living and tastelessness were abroad in the land. 'These blessings,' he said, 'shan't ruin me —by God, I'll ruin them!'—and he left his allotment to others and sailed off. Debtors endure demands, taxation, slavery, forced sales— they persevere too, feeding winged Harpies just as Phineus did, that steal and ravage their substance. These buy their corn before it is harvested and market the oil before the olives are picked. 'I take the wine too,' he says, 'at so much'—and he gives an advance on the price, while the bunch hangs on the vine and grows as it waits for Arcturus and the vintage.

Much of this recalls *Quiet of Mind*: the medical imagery, the

---

[27] *Odyssey* 5.264.   [28] ibid. 5.439.   [29] ibid. 5.291, 295.

Crates anecdote. Much however has a livelier tone. The tradition of popular preaching reveals itself in the range of rhetorical devices. Imagined interruptions, rhetorical questions, direct addresses to the audience, striking word-arrangements (asyndeta for instance) are characteristic. So is a certain vulgar vigour in the imagery: the fable of the vomiting vultures, the parable of paying a man to cut off your hand if it has gone rotten.[30] The moralised Homer too falls into the tradition, with its appeal to the one book the half-educated will know. The rapid transitions and vivid word-pictures recall Roman satire, which itself owes much to the traditions of Hellenistic preaching. Horace or Juvenal would not have been ashamed of the ending.

There were also occasions that demanded a grander manner. We possess a group of speeches which are very typically Plutarchan but exhibit yet a third mode: the grandeur of the ceremonial sophistic display. In one of these, *The Glory of Athens*, he argues a case which is of particular interest in view of some of his general ideas and attitudes. The position to be maintained is that Athenian achievements in practical affairs are greater than in literature. This chimes with a theme which is prominent in the *Parallel Lives*—the theme that Greece too had a political greatness and could share dominion with Rome as a useful partner. Thoroughly implausible as this thesis is, it had some point in the age of the first Eastern consuls.[31] Delivered at Athens in the late first century A.D., the speech would not be so absurd: less absurd anyway than those conventional praises of Marathon which Sulla told the Athenian orators to take home with them.[32]

The speech is very formal. The poets and generals of Athens come forward in turn. Finally comes the turn of the orators.

Poetry, you may say, is only a game. But a comparison between orators and generals has a certain plausibility. Does not Aeschines humorously represent Demosthenes as saying that he would take out an action on

[30] cf. Matthew 5.29–30; not the only coincidence between this piece and the Gospels: 830B recalls Matthew 6.26.
[31] cf. above, p. 9.　　　　[32] *Sulla* 13.4.

behalf of the Front Bench against the Headquarters? Well: is it right
to prefer Hyperides' speech on Plataea to Aristides' proclamation? Or
Lysias' speech against the Thirty to the tyrannicide of Thrasybulus
and Archinus? Or Aeschines' prosecution of Timarchus for male
prostitution to Phocion's expedition in aid of Byzantium, by which he
saved allies' sons from becoming victims of the drunken wantonness of
the Macedonians? Shall we set Demosthenes' speech on the Crown
against the crowns that Conon won for liberating Greece? The finest
and most eloquent thing the great orator did in that speech was the oath
by those of our ancestors who risked their lives at Marathon. He didn't
swear by those who taught lessons to boys in school! These were
therefore the people—not an Isocrates or an Antiphon or an Isaeus—
whom the city buried at public cost, welcoming home their bodily
remains; these were the people whom the orator in this oath treated as
gods, whom he swore by—but did not follow! Isocrates said that the
men who risked their lives at Marathon fought 'as though their lives
were not their own',[33] and praised their daring and contempt for life in
lyrical terms. But what of himself? When he was an old man, so the
story goes, someone asked him how he passed the time. 'Like a man
over ninety,' he said, 'who thinks death the greatest of evils.' For he
grew old not putting an edge on his sword or sharpening his lance, not
polishing a helmet, not soldiering or rowing in the galleys, but sticking
together antitheses, parisoses and homoeoptota, smoothing and shaping
his periods, as it were, with plane and chisel. How could the man who
was afraid to make vowel collide with vowel or utter an isocolon one
syllable short fail to be frightened of the noise of arms and the clash of
battalions? Miltiades set off for Marathon; next day he fought the
battle and returned victorious to the city with his army. Pericles
reduced Samos in nine months, and thought himself a finer fellow than
Agamemnon who took Troy in the tenth year of siege. And Isocrates
took nearly three Olympiads to write the *Panegyric*! In all that time he
fought no campaign, went on no embassy, founded no city, never
sailed in command of a fleet. Yet the age produced innumerable wars
. . . and all the time Isocrates was sitting at home, fashioning and re-
fashioning the phrases of a book, for as long as it took Pericles to build
the Propylaea and the Parthenon. Yet Cratinus[34] ridicules Pericles for
being so slow with his works; he says about the middle wall:

[33] Isocrates, *Panegyricus* 86.
[34] A poet of Old Comedy: fr. 300κ.

Pericles
advances it with speeches, but the work does not progress.

Just think of the sophistic pedantry that can spend the ninth part of a
lifetime on a single speech! (350B–351A)

Paradoxical of course that an orator should so denigrate his own
profession; but to make a case is not to commit oneself to it, and
we need not take this aspect of the speech too seriously. What is
characteristically Plutarchan is once again the range and aptness
of the examples. Here, his immense reading subserves purely
rhetorical purposes. The apt quotation from Aeschines makes an
ingenious amplification of the imaginary objection with which the
piece begins. The four parallel achievements of orators and
generals are neat and artful. No boredom is allowed here: after
Hyperides and Lysias comes the longer and more piquant matter
of male seduction, and finally the allusion to *On the Crown* which
leads by association to a further point. This is something very
traditional: a comment on the famous oath of which we possess
Longinus' model analysis.[35] Plutarch draws two little lessons:
(*i*) that Demosthenes chose soldiers, not rhetors, to personify the
greatness of his country;[36] (*ii*) that he himself did not practise
what he preached. The episode leads, through a parallel reference
to Marathon, to a much easier target: Isocrates. Plutarch has
again a tradition to draw on in the amusing passage that follows:[37]
Isocrates is the typical study-orator, who took absurdly long
periods of time furbishing and re-furbishing his work. The final
touch is ingenious and appropriate. The *Panegyricus* took as long
as the Parthenon, and even Pericles (though not in this connection!) was blamed for being slow. Plutarch recalls a piece of
antiquarian learning associated with a passage of Old Comedy.[38]

These three passages show a difference of mode, but a basic

---

[35] Demosthenes 18.208; 'Longinus' 16.
[36] The point is underlined by the untranslatable conceit of *PROkinduneusantas*
('risked their lives') and *PROdidaskontas* ('taught lessons'), the *pro-* in the second
verb being trivial or meaningless.
[37] cf. Dionysius, *On the Forcefulness of Demosthenes* 4.
[38] cf. *Pericles* 13.5, and indeed the whole marvellous passage, 12–13.

similarity of material. The mass of learning, the rich vocabulary, the constant search for analogies and images, the anxiety for frequent thematic change, characterise a manner which genre-differences affect only to a very limited extent. But there are genre-differences. Besides the kinds of speeches and treatises we have illustrated, there are, for example, the books of *problēmata* on antiquarian and scientific subjects, and the more technical philosophical treatises. In all these, there is less scope for brilliant play of *exempla* or quotations: the richness and the metaphorical style remain pervasive. The Lives, again, have many of the features of history: yet again and again a twist of argument or a series of anecdotes reveals the same techniques of allusion and illusion. Plutarch, it is true, has *l'âme de la naïveté*; but in style, he has a sophistication and cunning which make interpretation a continuously exacting task.

The most complex genre he attempted was the dialogue. Here lay his highest literary ambitions.

Philosophical dialogue is one of the great inventions of Greek literature, a proper expression and symbol of free inquiry. It took many forms. Some dialogues, like many of Plato's, consist of a rapid interchange of question and answer. Others are made up of a series of developed speeches giving various answers to the questions proposed; the less plausible answers usually come first, and are refuted in the course of the later speeches. Plutarch's dialogues are of the second kind; he rarely attempts the other. The tradition of this kind of dialogue also did in fact begin with Plato: impressive speeches occur in *Ion*, *Phaedo*, *Gorgias*, *Republic*, for example; *Symposium*, *Phaedrus*, *Timaeus* and *Laws*, with their solemnity and pomp, had very great influence on later practitioners. Aristotle, Theophrastus and their Hellenistic successors wrote many elaborate and famous dialogues; what they were like can be glimpsed, if at all, through the extant masters, Cicero and Plutarch.[39]

---

[39] No general history of the dialogue has yet replaced R. Hirzel, *Der Dialog* (1895). It is vital to remember that Aristotle (*Poetics* 1447b) was prepared to subsume the Socratic dialogue under poetry.

Plato's *Symposium,* an acknowledged masterpiece, has four features which were of special importance for the development of the genre. One is its dinner-setting, an ideally closed and conventional occasion, based on a social event which seems to have changed very little in character, in the circles that matter, between classical Athens and imperial Rome. A second is the device of using reported conversation to distance the event in time, lend credibility to the report, and incidentally involve more persons in the compliment of being included. A third, more conspicuous here than in any other Platonic dialogue, is the accommodation of style to profession and character, as in the speeches of Eryximachus, Aristophanes and Agathon. Finally, Alcibiades' drunken entry adds the interest of event to that of conversation. All these features recur in Plutarch. His 'Seven Sages' meet at dinner. In *Table Talk* the dinner-table is the venue of a whole series of small dialogues. Elaborate play with reported conversation is a puzzling feature of *The Face in the Moon.* Plutarch has not much stylistic versatility; but he makes the Pythagorean Theanor in *Socrates' Sign* speak in an appropriately grand manner, and he characterises Pisias and Anthemion in *A Book of Love* by their words as much as by anything he says about them. In the use of incident, on the other hand, he goes much further than Plato. This was indeed not an innovation: Varro's informative dialogue on farming startles us with the unexpected episode of the sacristan's murder.[40] But *Socrates' Sign* and *A Book of Love* are particularly striking, with their exciting novel-like settings and interludes. Indeed, the likeness between *A Book of Love,* where a narrated love-affair forms the background to a philosophical discussion, and, say, the first book of the novelist Achilles Tatius, where the love-affair in the story occasions general discourses by the characters, is remarkably close. In this kind of thing, the dialogue made a contribution to the development of the novel.

Certain of Plutarch's dialogues have historical, not contemporary, settings. *The Banquet of the Seven Sages* (146B ff.) is set in the Greece of the tyrants. Some have thought it too trivial for

[40] Varro, *De Re Rustica,* 1.59.2.

Plutarch's hand. One gets the impression of an educational work, addressed to a very young audience, full of instructive and amusing stories. The themes are in fact typically Plutarchan ones: the contribution of Delphi to Greek civilisation, the virtues of the simple life, prophecy, the value of a plain diet. As a myth, it has Herodotus' story of Arion and the dolphin, introduced as a piece of news brought by Periander's brother Gorgos and beautifully told. We know (14E) that Plutarch admired certain Hellenistic dialogues as introductory works for the young; he is here, it would seem, writing one on his own account.

Socrates' Sign (575A) is a more serious affair, though not dissimilar in its variety, and again involving, though on a deeper level, the themes of simplicity of life and the power of divination. This time Plutarch chose a more precise and factual historical setting, the liberation of Thebes from the Spartan occupation in 379 B.C. It was a famous tale of adventure, of which many accounts existed. Plutarch needed it also in *Pelopidas*, where he tells it more briefly. In the dialogue, there is much more detail, most of it no doubt traditional; he also takes the kind of liberty a Greek dramatist might take, compressing the whole crisis into the events of a single day and night. The dialogue (like the *Banquet*) is a narrated one: the Theban Caphisias relates it to an Athenian sympathiser at Athens. The principal scene of his story is in the house of Simmias, the disciple known from Plato's *Phaedo*, now a bedridden elder. Friends are in the habit of assembling here, during the occupation, for philosophical and conspiratorial talk. It is the wintry day when the exiles are to slip into the town from the mountains, and the coup against the occupation forces is to be mounted. Coincidence—an implausibility on which the unity of the dialogue is based—has brought to Thebes at this very time a mysterious stranger, who is reported to have camped near the tomb of the Pythagorean Lysis. The two sets of events thus set in train, one public, the other private and philosophical, are linked by the person of the young Epaminondas, the boy who was to be the greatest of Theban heroes. He plays no active part in the conspiracy, though he knows about it; his inaction needs an apologia. In his relation with the mysterious stranger, who turns out to be a Pythagorean 'holy man', a colourful and somewhat pompous figure, he gives proof both of his steadfast integrity and of supernatural guidance, which the wise man recognises. Developments in these two plots punctuate the discussions which occupy the main part of the dialogue; it is the theory contained in these discussions which is obviously the most important part of the whole. The news of the stranger's ritual acts prompts the rationally-inclined Galaxidorus to deliver an attack on superstition. Socrates, he suggests, appealing to Simmias, championed a simple, down-to-earth philosophy.

But what about the 'divine sign', so celebrated in Socratic literature? The ensuing conversation consists of the discussion of a series of explanations of this, interrupted from time to time by news of what is going on outside. Was it a sneeze? A voice? The voiceless language of a *daimon*? This last is Simmias' explanation; it is a theme which Plutarch takes up in a number of other dialogues written about this time. As a Delphic priest and a man of learning, the theology of prophecy was central to his interests. Simmias is made to crown his explanation, in the Platonic manner, by a myth: the story of Timarchus of Chaeronea, who descended into the cave of the near-by oracle of Trophonius and had a vision of heaven and of the destiny and nature of the soul. This splendid story concluded, the Pythagorean adds his *ex cathedra* word; and the moment for action has come.

So varied a subject naturally requires many variations of style. The myth and Theanor's closing speech have distinct and fascinating forms of grandeur. The narrative too is among the best in Plutarch. It shows qualities not revealed in the arabesques of allusion and analogy: a clear eye for action, a powerful technique of suspense, the natural skill of the born story-teller.

It was late. The wind had risen, and the cold was sharper. Most people had hurried home. We met Damoclidas, Pelopidas and Theopompus [exiles] and took them with us. Others brought in others. They had become separated crossing Cithaeron. The weather enabled them to wrap up and conceal their faces so as to cross the city without apprehension. As some of them passed through the gate, there was lightning on their right, but no thunder. It seemed a good omen of security and glory, signifying a brilliant but safe action.

All forty-eight of us were already indoors, and Theocritus was sacrificing privately in a separate room, when there was a violent beating on the door. Presently someone came to say that two of Archias' servants were knocking at the outer door. They had been sent in haste to Charon, demanded entry, and were angry at the delay in answering. Charon was dumbfounded. He gave orders to open up at once, and himself went to meet these servants with his garland on, as though he had sacrificed and was drinking, and asked them what they wanted. 'Archias and Philip,' said one of them, 'sent us to ask you to come and see them as quickly as possible.' Charon asked what the urgency was in a summons at such an hour. Was there any new development? 'We know nothing more,' said the man; 'what are we to tell them?' 'That I'm coming,' said Charon, 'as soon as I've taken off my garland and put on my cloak. If I come with you at this hour, I shall cause a disturbance with some people, because they will think I am being arrested.' 'Very well,' said the man, 'you do that. We've orders from the governors to the guard in the lower town.'

They thereupon departed, and Charon came back to us and told us. Universal dismay; we thought we must have been betrayed.

However, all agreed that Charon should go and obey the governors' summons. (594D–595A)

And so Charon goes, leaving his fifteen-year-old son as a pledge of his loyalty. The conspirators get more and more anxious, and decide to go out and fight, rather than be scraped out like a wasps' nest.

While we were arming and getting ready, Charon returned. Cheerful and smiling, he gave us a look, and told us not to worry. There was no crisis, everything was going according to plan. He told his story.

'By the time I had answered their call, Archias and Philip were exceedingly drunk. Neither their minds nor their bodies were capable of much. They managed with difficulty to get up and come out to the door. "It's the exiles," said Archias; "we hear they've got into the town and are in hiding." "Where?" said I, thoroughly confused, "and who are they supposed to be?" "We don't know," said Archias; "that's why we've sent for you, in case you've heard anything more definite."

'I began to recover from the shock. I reckoned their information could only be a vague rumour ... If anyone with knowledge had given information, they could hardly have failed to know the house ... So I replied, "I know there were a lot of idle reports around that caused us trouble while Androclides was alive. But I've not heard anything at the moment, Archias. However, I'll look into it, if you like, and if I hear anything worth thinking about, it shan't escape you." ' (595ꜰ–596ʙ)

Reassured, the conspirators sally forth in two parties.

It was the time people are generally at dinner. The wind had got up stronger, and was blowing snow with it mixed with fine rain. The streets were empty as we passed through them ... But our bad luck, that was always evening out the odds between the enemy's ignorance and cowardice and our courage and care, complicating our action from the very beginning with episodes of danger like a play—our bad luck joined us again right at the climax and gave us a sharp and fearsome bout and an unexpected turn.

While Charon, having calmed Archias and Philip, had returned home and was organizing us for the action, a letter arrived from Athens, from the hierophant Archias to our Archias, his friend. This letter, it appears, announced the return and conspiracy of the exiles, the house where they had assembled, and the names of their confederates. But by this time Archias was thoroughly under the effects of his drink, and also excited by the prospect of the women.[41] He took the letter, but when the courier said it was about a serious matter, he replied 'Serious matters to-morrow', put the letter under his cushion, asked for another cup, and kept sending Phyllidas to the door to see if the ladies were coming.

These prospects kept the party going. Meanwhile, we had arrived and pushed our way past the servants to the dining-room. We stood at the door for a time, taking in the guests. The sight of our garlands and dresses gave the necessary false impression of our visit, and produced silence. Melon was the first to spring forward, hand on sword-hilt. Cabirichus, the archon-by-lot, gripped his arm as he passed and called out, 'Phyllidas, isn't this Melon?' Melon shook him off and pulled out his sword. Archias struggled to his feet, but Melon was on top of him and didn't stop striking till he had killed him. Philip was wounded in

[41] Women had been promised; they were in fact the conspirators in disguise.

the neck by Charon, but tried to defend himself with the drinking-cups on the table, until Lysitheus pushed him off the couch on to the ground and killed him . . . A few of the servants tried to resist, but we killed them. Those who made no fuss we locked up in the dining-room, not wanting them to get out and spread the word of what had happened until we knew whether our comrades had been successful. (596C–597D)

The other party, headed by Pelopidas, are at the house of Leontiades.

They told the servant . . . they had come from Athens with a letter . . . He gave the message and was told to open up. When he took the bar out and opened the door a little, they all tumbled in, threw the man down and rushed through the courtyard into the bedroom. Leontiades guessed the truth, drew his dagger and prepared to resist. Wicked tyrant that he was, he was a courageous man and strong in the arm. However, he did not think of overturning the lamp and confronting his enemies in the darkness. In the light he could be seen. The moment the door opened, he struck Cephisodorus in the side, and then fell on Pelopidas and shouted for the servants. Samidas and his companions however prevented them from doing anything; they had no stomach for joining issue with distinguished citizens of such superior fighting power. Pelopidas however had a real sword-fight with Leontiades in the narrow doorway of the bedroom. Cephisodorus had fallen in the way and was dying, so that the others could not get in to help. In the end, though, our man, who was wounded in the head, though not seriously, and had given as much as he had received, threw Leontiades and killed him over the still warm body of Cephisodorus, who saw his enemy fall and gave Pelopidas his hand and saluted the others before dying, a happy man. (597D–F)

This is not the end; but the remaining episodes, the murder of Hypatas on the roof and the release of political prisoners from the gaol, add little to the essentials.

These scenes of indoor violence owe much to the *Odyssey*, on which Plutarch's readers will have been brought up. Much of the detail is of course traditional, and perhaps very little is complete invention. But the choice and arrangement are special to the occasion. *Pelopidas* (10–11) shows some interesting differences, some of which follow naturally from the difference between Caphisias' narrative and the omniscient historian's. When Charon returns from his alarming interview, he tells only Pelopidas, or Pelopidas and his immediate group, the truth, but makes up another tale for the rest. This would not do for Caphisias: how could he have known? The version in the Life also emphasises Pelopidas' importance, as does its account of the death of Leontiades, which is represented as much the harder prong of the operation. Cephisodorus' dying words are not allowed either; he is quite dead, and Pelopidas fights on his own.

The differences are small but significant. The episode makes a good test for reflection on Plutarch's skills. Its vividness is not commonplace in ancient literature; it reminds us that Plutarch could write, better than most Greeks of his age, with his eye on the object, as well as out of the ready resources of a well-stocked literary memory.

CHAPTER THREE

The Scholar and his Books

Such then are some of the patterns; of what threads was the web woven? We must try next to form some view of what Plutarch read, and of the spirit and criteria with which he assessed it.

First, one or two general remarks.

The conditions of scholarship in ancient times were very different from those that prevail today, and this in itself is apt to interpose a barrier to understanding. We have indexes and reference-books, especially complete in classical studies; Plutarch had hardly anything like this. The inconvenience of looking up passages in papyrus rolls is almost too obvious to mention. The trained and constantly exercised memory of the ancient man of letters played a larger part than we can easily imagine.

The field to be covered was immense. 'Of making many books there is no end'[1] is a heartfelt cry in the Hellenistic world. To us, classical literature is a countable number of texts; this is the accident of time, it was not so for Plutarch. Even the libraries of Athens that he longed for when he was at home in Chaeronea contained only a chance selection of the enormous possibilities. Yet, apart from the acknowledged classics, few books existed in many copies. Instead, we should envisage countless different titles, each circulating in a small range, and many more or less duplicating one another. With few exceptions, we can hardly speak of a standard history or commentary. Quite small local groups would each have their own. It follows that an individual scholar could only hope to see a few of the books that he had heard of; and from this it was inevitable that he should often

[1] *Ecclesiastes* 12.12.

repeat opinions and references at second or third hand. To be able to cite impressive references (*marturia*) conferred prestige. The situation even gave rise to elaborate jokes and swindles, of which the *Minor Parallels* attributed to Plutarch offers a specimen.[2] Even Plutarch, who was both honest and intelligent, may sometimes have been taken in.

In a sense, this was an unspecialised culture. Plutarch's range was extraordinarily wide. History, philosophy, physics, botany, zoology, mathematics, grammar are all parts of his unified learning. At first sight it is like the range of an Aristotle, and it is of course true that all later Greek culture owed an enormous amount to the tradition of universality inherited from Aristotle, and from the even more remote days of the early sophists. But the universality was won at a price. Hellenistic science and Hellenistic philology had both been great achievements. But they stopped growing at a point short of the development of specialised and exclusive disciplines. This pause in scientific creativity is no doubt related to the diffusion and effectiveness of a uniform grammatical, rhetorical and moral education. Plutarch, the great traditionalist and educator, naturally reflects this situation very clearly. He did not seek the intellectual frontiers. His activity and his writing show very much the syndrome we might expect: wide-ranging knowledge, not only in literature and history but in mathematics and science, organised according to the patterns of thinking which the teaching of *rhetor* and *grammaticus* had made instinctive, and converted thereby into a powerful instrument of social and moral education.

The general aim of purveying moral education through learning can of course be attempted on many different levels. Plutarch's appeal was to the highly-trained, the imaginative, the leisured. He was not offering a short cut. He wrote for those who could appreciate the web of allusion and reminiscence which he spun out of his learning. And it was out of his books and the

[2] 305A ff. Quintilian (1.8.21) speaks of those who invent authorities with security, because 'those who never existed cannot be discovered'. See R. Syme, *Ammianus and the Historia Augusta*, 118 ff.

bookish conversations of his côterie that he created a valid medium in which to present a civilisation.

It would be simple-minded indeed to regard *Table Talk* as realistic, but this after all is how Plutarch and his friends liked to be thought of. According to one of these little dialogues (675D), a party of these people was entertained once at dinner in Corinth by the arch-priest Lucanius. They discussed why the prize at the Isthmian games was a pine-garland. A guide (*periēgētēs*) gave the standard mythological explanation of how Melicertes' body was found on the shore near a pine-tree. The question then arose why the pine should be associated with Poseidon and Dionysus. Plutarch makes various points: both gods are concerned with a 'liquid element'; pines are used for shipbuilding, and places where they grow are also good for vines.

When this had been said, one of the *rhētores* who was reputed to be the most deeply versed in liberal readings [*eleutheria anagnōsmata*], burst out.

'Good God! Wasn't it only the other day that the pine became the garland at the Isthmia? They used surely to use celery. We can see this from the words of the miser in the comedy:

> I'd gladly sell the Isthmian games
> for what the celery garland fetches.

The historian Timaeus also tells us that when the Corinthians were marching to fight the Carthaginians for Sicily, some asses carrying celery appeared in their way.[3] Most of the army took it as a bad omen, because celery has associations with funerals and we say that anyone dangerously ill "is in need of celery". But Timoleon found various ways of giving them confidence—especially by reminding them of the celery at the Isthmus with which the Corinthians crown victors. And there was Antigonus' flagship that was named *Isthmia* because celery sprouted on the stern. And there's the drinking-song [*skolion*] . . . that runs:

> The soil of Kōlias, scorched in the fire,
> hides the god Dionysus' dark-red blood,
> and carries Isthmian sprigs about its lip.

[3] cf. *Timoleon* 26.

Haven't you read this . . .?'

This made an impression on the young men, who thought him a very learned and well-read person.

Lucanius looked at me and smiled.

'Poseidon!' he said, 'what a quantity of literature! I suppose the people who have been persuading us of the opposite theory have been taking advantage of our ignorance and lack of reading! On their view, the pine was the original garland of the games, but the foreign celery came in from Nemea because of Heracles and totally superseded it as a suitable religious symbol. But then as time went on the pine recovered its old privilege and now flourishes in high repute. For my part, I was convinced by this, and listened carefully, so as actually to memorise and retain many of the references [*marturia*]. One was a passage of Euphorion on Melicertes[4] . . . Another was Callimachus, who was more explicit and makes Heracles say something about celery . . . And I fancy I have also come across a book by Procles on the Isthmian Games, in which he says that they held the first competition for a garland of pine, but when it was made a sacred contest they took over the celery garland from the Nemean festival. This Procles was a student at the Academy with Xenocrates.' (676c–677b)

This is a simple dramatisation of a question posed, a *probléma*. Such discussions of specific and defined questions not linked in connected argument are very common at all periods in the history of ancient learning. Aristotle and his successors treated all kinds of topics in this way, and Plutarch clearly knew the Aristotelian collection of *problémata* much as we have it. In *Greek Questions*, *Roman Questions* and *Natural Questions* he reproduces the Aristotelian form. A question is propounded, alternative answers are put forward, with evidence from authorities where possible. The most favoured solution usually comes last. In *Table Talk*, the form is lightly dramatised; learning comes out of the study and confers prestige at the dinner-table. The form indeed provides a framework which can be used even in a more elaborate and dramatic dialogue: the skeleton of *Socrates' Sign* after all is a set of

---

[4] A passage of five obscure lines follows: Euphorion, fr. 84 Powell. The Callimachus passage which follows is from the *Aitia*: fr. 59 Pfeiffer.

alternative answers to the question what the 'sign' was. Similarly in historical matters; we shall see the same sort of thing in the *Lives*.

This little passage quotes a comedy, two historians, a *skolion*, two Alexandrian poets, and an obscure fourth-century philosopher-antiquarian. It naturally makes us ask how extensive Plutarch's reading really was.

The evidence which it is easiest to use for this question is that of the quotations, of which his extant works contain some seven thousand. By no means all of these are from first-hand reading. He drew, as we have seen, on prepared sets of extracts, and he collected excerpts and commonplaces for himself. We have no good rules for distinguishing the second-hand from the first-hand; perhaps indeed it is not a very significant distinction. We may however remember that collections and anthologies were not as a rule selections chosen for literary excellence, as they usually are nowadays: they were more likely to be composed of sets of extracts on particular themes—'virtue' or 'old age' for instance —like the enormous compilation of Stobaeus, which tells us so much about the interests of those who pillaged the classics for educational purposes. Or again, passages were collected by *rhetores* and grammarians to illustrate rhetorical or stylistic techniques. These too would stick in the mind. It might seem that a quotation used not for its content but as mere stylistic variation has a somewhat better chance of coming from a memory of actual reading. But even this is a perilous path; it may after all be an anthology passage committed to memory for another purpose. If we were to assume that everything that might possibly have come through an intermediary in fact did so, Plutarch's own primary reading need not have been so very large. What inclines one to a more generous estimate is above all the richness and allusiveness of his own 'mosaic' style. It is not only when he is quoting that he gives proof of his vast acquaintance with all kinds of books.

Some things hardly need proof.[5] Among classical poets,

[5] W. C. Helmbold—E. N. O'Neil, *Plutarch's Quotations*, 1959, forms a basis for the study of this side of Plutarch's work; much remains to be done.

Plutarch was familiar with Homer, with more plays of the tragedians and of Menander than we have, and with a good deal of lyric poetry. References to Archilochus and Simonides suggest some special concern with them. He had at his finger-tips also a fair amount of hexameter poetry which is difficult to identify; probably it is mostly Alexandrian. Plutarch was apparently well read in the Alexandrians: not only in Nicander and Aratus, with their quasi-scientific subject matter, on whom he commented, but in Callimachus and Euphorion as well. It is a reasonable conjecture that he liked their sophistication and elegance.[6]

For another reason, he was specially attracted to Hesiod and Pindar: they were Boeotian and Plutarch had a strong local patriotism. He wrote a life of Pindar, now lost. *A priori* one would expect him to be steeped in the poems. The evidence of the quotations is not so clear. There are about thirty references to the *Victory Odes*, the only poems that survive entire. Some of these at any rate are typically second-hand. 'Corinthus was the son of Zeus'[7] is a proverbial boast. 'Higher than any business'[8] is mediated through Plato and is a prefatory commonplace for putting learned discussion (*scholē*) above the business of the world (*ascholia*). 'Precinct of deep-warring Ares'[9] was a phrase Pindar used of Syracuse; Plutarch uses it of Rome; he uses it moreover in the life of the conqueror of Syracuse, yet without making any attempt to draw piquancy or irony from the original context. What makes one think it second-hand, however, is not this absence of contextual association—that is quite normal in ancient authors—but the fact that Plutarch quotes in the same context a whole group of similar phrases describing warlike cities. Such useful material for writers of encomia is likely to have been collected for that purpose.

It is often said that Plutarch knew the *Hymns* and other poems better than the *Victory Odes*. Here of course we are without

---

[6] e.g. 567E for Nicander; *Antony* 70 for Callimachus—the story of the misanthrope Timon is attached to the interpretation of an epigram; 911F, lines of Aratus introduced in a purely scientific *problēma*.
[7] *Nem.* 7.105 = 1072B.   [8] *Isthm.* 1.2 = 575D.
[9] *Pyth.* 2.1 = *Marcellus* 21.

control. Once again, there are a number of passages which could have occurred in collections illustrating specific points: the nature of time, freedom from care, Zeus the great craftsman.[10] Others are commonplaces of a different order: 'heart forged of adamant or iron'[11] is a way of saying 'inflexible'. One very splendid passage,[12] which Plutarch quotes three times, happens to illustrate a notorious irregularity of syntax: was it for this that it stuck in the mind?

We should, I think, accept that Plutarch knew and loved his Pindar; we cannot say that the manner or number of his quotations clinches it.

Not only the provenance, but the effect, of a quotation often raises difficult questions. Plutarch's father in *A Book of Love* (762D) makes a simple point with a wealth of allusion:

But surely love makes grumpy and disagreeable people kinder and pleasanter.

'When the fire's ablaze, the house makes a better impression,'[13]

and a man is more cheerful when love's heat warms him. But most people react very oddly. When they see a glare in the house at night, they think it miraculous and marvel. But when they see a small, mean, ignoble mind suddenly filled with pride, liberty, ambition, grace and generosity, they feel no compulsion to say with Telemachus

'Indeed there is some god within.'[14]

And here is another thing, Daphnaeus, that is surely supernatural. The lover despises almost everything—friends and family, laws, rulers and kings: he neither fears nor admires nor courts. He can endure

'even the lightning with its spear.'[15]

But let him but catch sight of his beloved, and

'like a beaten cock, he drops his wing',[16]

his confidence is smashed, the pride of his heart is broken.

---

[10] Fragments 33, 52d.50 ff., 57 Snell.   [11] Fragment 123 Snell.
[12] Fragment 70b, 10–11 Snell.
[13] *Contest of Homer and Hesiod* 273 = pseudo-Herodotus, *Life of Homer* 31; cf. also 100D.
[14] *Odyssey* 19.40.   [15] Pindar, *Pyth.* 1.5.   [16] Phrynichus, fr. 17 Nauck.

This is of course a typical passage of allusive ornament. The quotations are not used for support or authority; they lend colour and dignity. (*i*) Love is compared to fire, and this provides a meaningful link between the first two quotations. The first of these is a proverbial one: fire is one of the good things of life; by implication, love is another. The second brings to mind the scene in *Odyssey* xix, where Odysseus and Telemachus collect the armour and are guided miraculously by Athene with a lamp. This works by contrast: Telemachus realised there was a god somewhere about as any ordinary person would in the circumstances; the psychological miracle of love produces no such comment from jaded and blinkered mankind. (*ii*) The new point, the fearlessness of the lover, whom nothing but his beloved can put out of countenance, is again enlivened by two quotations. This time there is no link between them. Pindar, in the magnificent prelude of the First Pythian, was illustrating the power of song. The lightning's 'spear' is thus here a purely stylistic ornament; no contextual load is transferred with it. We may guess it came from direct memory of Pindar, not through any anthology. The tragedian's image of the fighting-cock which follows is more difficult to evaluate. We do not know to what the early tragedian Phrynichus, if indeed it was he, first applied it. Plutarch uses it once in a military context, and once[17] of Alcibiades' erotic submission to Socrates—a situation which exactly exemplifies the one in our passage. Now it is unlikely that Plutarch read Phrynichus. On the other hand, it seems probable, to judge from the nature of the image itself, that it was originally about fighting and not about love. Yet the parallel with the passage about Alcibiades suggests that at some stage the line acquired an erotic association. If this is so, it brings this with it to the context we are considering.

The other Boeotian classic, Hesiod, was even closer to Plutarch's heart than Pindar. Plutarch compiled a four-book commentary on the *Works and Days*, something of which can be reconstructed from later comment which incorporated it. We get the impression of a strongly moralistic work, in which the

[17] *Alcibiades* 4.3.

scholarship and science are harnessed to a clearly defined educational purpose. Hesiod wrote:

> The eye of Zeus, that sees all and notices all,
> sees this too if he pleases, it does not escape him,
> the sort of justice that goes within this city.
> May I not be just among men,
> nor my son either; it is bad to be just
> if the unjuster has the greater share.
> But Zeus the lightning-hurler will not bring this to pass. (267–73)

'Unworthy of Hesiod's view about justice and injustice', says Plutarch (fr. 38), deleting the whole passage, the ironical tone of which he entirely fails to see. Again:

> At the mouth of a river that flows into the sea
> or at a spring, never make water or relieve yourself:
> be careful of this! (757–9)

'Vulgar and unworthy of educational poetry', he says, and strikes the lines out (fr. 98). Positive interpretations too are often moralising: 'I will speak to you in good will' (286) is said to illustrate 'the philosophical character'; 'Archilochus and Hipponax wrote invectives against those who injured them . . . but Hesiod, the true man of the muses (*mousikos*) . . . admonishes his brother, from whom he suffered injury, but does not vilify him' (fr. 40). Moral criticism passes sometimes into aesthetic, in a way which reminds us how close the two spheres were in ancient thinking. Plutarch notes the passage:

> Dawn, whose coming sets many men upon their way (580–1).

Homer, he observes, uses epithets of charm for 'dawn': she is 'saffron-robed' or 'rosy-fingered'. Hesiod 'in grander vein' (*meizonōs*) takes his cue from the work to which dawn summons men as she goes forth (fr. 79). The contrast between charm, which is associated with pleasure, and grandeur with its associated moral worth, is the fundamental one with which Greco-Roman literary appreciation operates. Plutarch is here making the claim that

Hesiod belongs to a higher category of poet than Homer; he is more serious, more useful to the community.

At the same time, the commentary is not just moralising: it contains a good deal of learning, both philological and scientific. Any commentary is a natural habitat for *problēmata*. Is the 'house-carrier' (78) a snail or, as some held, a small insect like a bee that gathers rubbish for its winter nest? Why (497) does Hesiod speak of the swollen foot of a starving man? This has, says Plutarch, a scientific explanation. Lack of food forces our bodily heat to consume some portion of the body itself, but the strength to digest what is consumed is lacking. The upper parts of the body there-fore become emaciated, while the undigested material taken from them goes to swell the lower limbs.

The moralising in the Hesiod commentary would be more sur-prising if we did not possess a work in which Plutarch laid down the general principles of the educational interpretation of poetry. *On Reading the Poets* (14D) was written, ostensibly at least, for his own needs and a friend's, confronted with the problem of their son's literary education. It is ultimately based on Plato's rules for the exclusion of immoral myths from the ideal society;[18] but Plutarch also uses later educational works, and he cannot of course acquiesce in Plato's exclusion of poetry from an educational system of which it was a fundamental part. Plato had pushed a view of human reason to an extreme conclusion; Plutarch is responding to an actual educational problem. His response must seem timid and prudish; it is hard to believe that Homer and Menander presented much danger to the young people of Chae-ronea. But the problem is a real one, and is after all always with us. Two things should be said on Plutarch's behalf: that he does not give interpretations which he believes to be untrue; and that the moral propositions of whose certainty he is convinced are those of a humane and civilised person.

The book uses a whole technique of interpretation, which goes back to Peripatetic and Alexandrian criticism. Confronted by a 'difficult' passage, we can turn to a number of lines of attack:

[18] *Republic* II and III.

context, the character of the speaker, obscure word-usage, the possibility of allegory, the inevitable limitations and conditions of the process of imitation (*mimēsis*). There is much shrewd observation, whether Plutarch's or a predecessor's. He notices for example that Homeric usage differs from later Greek:

The actual word *tuchē* (fortune) was not yet in use; but the poets were aware of the strength of the irregularly and indeterminately moving cause, and the inability of human reason to predict it; they therefore used the names of the gods to describe this—just as we use the adjectives 'supernatural' and 'divine' of events, moral qualities, speeches and men. Many apparently outrageous statements about Zeus are to be corrected in this manner: e.g. . . .

> For then the beginning of woe rolled forward
> for Trojans and Greeks, through mighty Zeus' design.[19]

. . . He means here Fortune or Fate, the element in causation unamenable to our calculations and in general outside our control. (24A ff.)

So Homer and Plato are reconciled! Plutarch also noted something which some recent scholarship[20] has emphasised and made much of: the shift in meaning of *aretē* ('virtue') from the 'nonmoral' to the 'moral'. Plutarch's explanation however is not historical; it is grammatical, and depends on the theory of tropes.

Aretē not only makes men wise, just and good in word and deed, but also commonly invests them with fame and power, and for this reason they regard fame and power as *aretē*. We may compare the use of 'olive' and 'beech' as homonyms to describe both the trees and for the fruit they bear. So when the poets say

> The gods have put sweat in the way of *aretē*[21]

. . . the young student should realize that this is said of the noblest and most divine quality in us, which we conceive as rightness of reason,

---

[19] *Iliad* 4.81. For the point Plutarch makes, cf. Macrobius, *Saturnalia* 5.16.
[20] e.g. A. W. H. Adkins, *Merit and Responsibility*. Adkins' views have been much discussed; compare H. Lloyd-Jones, *The Justice of Zeus*, 1971; A. A. Long, *JHS* 90 (1970) 121 ff.
[21] Hesiod, *Works and Days* 289; no doubt Plutarch's commentary contained similar observations.

excellence of our rational nature, and a consistent habit of mind. On the other hand when he reads . . .

> With wealth go *aretē* and glory,[22]

he must not sit back in wonder and amazement at the rich, as though *aretē* were something wealth could buy . . . he must realize that the poet has used *aretē* in the sense of reputation, power, success, or the like. (24c *ff.*)

With such educational views, it would be surprising if Plutarch's appreciation of some ranges of literature were not seriously inhibited. Comedy presented an obvious problem.

In *Table Talk* (711A) there is a discussion about the suitability of Old and New Comedy for convivial occasions. Old Comedy is found very unsuitable: it is too much in earnest, its humour is vulgar and obscene, every guest would need his personal commentator to explain the proper names. Menander on the other hand is excellent for the purpose. His style is pleasing and normal, he offers useful and simple *gnōmai*. His mixture of fun and seriousness is about right for people who have had a certain amount to drink. The love-interest also is appropriate: there is no homosexuality, and seductions usually end in marriage. This is just what suits dinner-guests who are going home to their wives afterwards.[23] Indeed, Menander's amiable elegance has a particular psychological value in a company relaxed over their wine: it diverts their humour in a civilised direction.[24]

And not only at dinner, as we learn from the *Comparison of Aristophanes and Menander*:

In the theatre, in the lecture-room, at the dinner-party, his poetry provides reading, study and entertainment for a wider public than that commanded by any other Greek masterpiece. He shows what mastery of language really is. He approaches every point with inescapable persuasiveness, and has under control every resource of sound and meaning that Greek affords. What good reason has an educated man

---

[22] *Works and Days* 313.
[23] Plutarch seems to be thinking of the guests who ride eagerly home to their wives at the end of Xenophon's *Symposium*.
[24] Compare the remark of F. H. Sandbach, *Oxford Classical Dictionary*, ed. 2, s.v. Menander: 'M. quietly inculcated humane virtues.'

for going to the theatre, except to see Menander? What else fills the
theatres with men of learning, when a comic character takes the
stage? (854A)

But even if Plutarch's outlook was too limited for him to
appreciate Old Comedy, he had reason to read it in connection
with his historical studies. What we cannot tell is how far he
browsed in the plays himself. If they were difficult and uncongenial, one would expect him to rely more on second-hand
references, on the 'dictionaries of persons mentioned in comedy'
(*kōmōdoumenoi*) of which we have some evidence.[25]

In any case, the great enterprise of the *Lives*, as it developed
in his hands, must have given him a stimulus to a wider and more
purposeful reading of anything bearing on history. It seems to
have been for this, for example, that he took to reading Latin,
of which he had, as he tells us, a practical knowledge which fell
short of appreciation of the qualities of Latin style, its 'beauty
and rapidity'.[26] This will be a reading knowledge; he will not
have needed much conversational Latin, for his Roman friends
would all speak Greek, and would indeed be ready enough to
instruct him on Roman matters. It was a competent but not
infallible knowledge: enough for quite rapid use of Sallust or
Nepos. It is wrong to underestimate it because Plutarch makes
mistakes.[27] And it is in connection with the *Lives* that the whole
question of the range and depth of his learning assumes most
urgency. As historians, we should very much like to know what
he had read and how he used it. Fortunately, the literary conventions of the *Lives* admit, or indeed require, a certain amount of
reference to sources and 'problematic' discussion of different
views. But Plutarch does not, as it were, give a bibliography. Few

---

[25] See below, p. 120 and note.
[26] *Demosthenes* 2.2. 'Rapidity' (*tachos*), is unexpected; the Romans thought
their language more measured than Greek (Seneca, *Epist.* 40.11), but one always
exaggerates a foreigner's speed of talking.
[27] In general, see H. Peter, *Die Quellen Plutarchs* ... (1865), 61. A characteristic carelessness is to be seen in *Marcellus* 30.4, compared with Valerius Maximus
5.1. ext. 6. For a less generous view of Plutarch's Latin, see C. P. Jones, *Plutarch
and Rome*, 81 ff; he is right to draw attention to the part which bilingual assistants
may have played in making Latin literature available.

ancient writers do; the first book of Pliny's *Natural History* is altogether exceptional. There is much we must assume: familiarity with the classical historians of Greece, Herodotus, Thucydides, Xenophon, Ephorus, Theopompus. There is much too that we cannot know. Plutarch must have had, for example, some general histories of Rome besides Dionysius on which he could rely for the main outlines of the events against which his heroes moved. There can be no doubt that he read Livy; but it hardly seems likely that so vast a work in Latin would be his first resource in need. Where he names his authorities is where there are differences to be reconciled. We thus know something of the principles on which he judged evidence—but only where he thought the discussion interesting or impressive. We have to guess from this what reading lies behind the unargued and undisputed narrative.

A good example of source-discussion is the opening chapter of *Aristides*,[28] a life which involved a fair amount of research and necessitated making a synthesis of the varied but not very abundant evidence.

Plutarch is always interested in the wealth of his heroes. The use of riches and the value of poverty are favourite moral themes; we may compare the reflections on Epaminondas embodied in *Socrates' Sign* (583D ff.). About Aristides there was a divergence of opinion. One authority was the Peripatetic Demetrius of Phalerum, who had discussed Aristides in a book on Socrates,[29] whose first wife Myrto was supposed to be a relative of Aristides. Demetrius argued that Aristides was quite well off, for three reasons: (*i*) because he was chosen as archon out of the highest property-class; (*ii*) because he was ostracised; (*iii*) because he dedicated a tripod in the theatre as choregus. Plutarch answers all these points, though not in the same order. The dedication of the tripod (*iii*) proves nothing. Notably poor persons like Epaminondas and Plato did this, because others bore the expense, and there is no reason why a good man should not accept this kind of

---

[28] cf. J. R. Hamilton, *Plutarch's 'Alexander'*, xlviii.
[29] Fragments 9–98 Wehrli (*Die Schule des Aristoteles*): fr. 102 is from a book on Aristides.

help. The Stoic philosopher Panaetius, the teacher of Posidonius, also no doubt in connection with Socrates, advanced a more antiquarian sort of argument: two other persons called Aristides had dedicated choregic offerings, but Demetrius was wrong in identifying the great statesman with either of these, because the alphabet used in these inscriptions was the reformed alphabet authorised in the archonship of Euclides at the end of the fifth century. Plutarch fails to discuss this point; it deserves 'further examination', he says. He relies rather on the argument of probability from the pious and impecunious Epaminondas. As to ostracism (*ii*), he points out that intellectual or oratorical fame might be sufficient ground even without great wealth: witness Damon of Oa, Pericles' *éminence grise*. The argument about the archonship (*i*) is again attacked on two fronts. The Epicurean Idomeneus had asserted that Aristides' archonship was by election not by lot. 'And,' adds Plutarch, 'if, as Demetrius himself says, it was after the battle of Plataea that he held the office, it is very plausible (*pithanon*) that, with his reputation so high and his successes so great, he should have been deemed worthy on account of merit (*aretē*) of an office which those who were success-ful in the lot attained by reason of wealth.' Now the facts seem to be these: Aristides was the archon who gave his name to the archon-year 489/8, long before Plataea; he *may* have held another archonship some other time; the use of the lot began shortly after, in 487/6; and at all times down to 457/6 the top *two* property classes, not the top *one*, were eligible. Plutarch's *pithanon* argu-ment needs careful interpretation. Later in the Life (5.9), he accepts the correction of Demetrius' date, on the ground that no Aristides is to be found in the archon lists after Plataea, though one is mentioned immediately after Phaenippus who was archon in the year of Marathon. He does not say whether Idomeneus used this fact. In the *pithanon* argument, therefore, he is not admitting the correctness of Demetrius' date; he is saying rather that, if this date is correct, it does not follow, as Demetrius wanted it to follow, that Aristides was wealthy. On the contrary his achievements might plausibly have earned him an honour normally put out to lot among the rich. Demetrius, however, could not have entertained this possibility; his obvious motive was 'to rescue both Aristides and Socrates from the imputation of what he regarded as the great evil of poverty'.

This is not the only controversy discussed in *Aristides*, and it is perhaps worth looking at one other, which raises somewhat different issues. In ch. 26, Plutarch mentions the account given by the late fourth-century Macedonian Craterus of a trial of Aristides for corruption in the assessment of the allies' tribute. Plutarch does not believe this. One reason is that Craterus usually adduces documents; indeed, his historical work apparently took the form of a collection of official Athenian documents with historical explanation. Secondly, nobody else mentions any such trial.[30] The argument that a minority of one cannot be right is one that Plutarch often adduces, usually in conjunction with other considerations. Here he reinforces it by remarking on the silence even of other writers who, like Craterus, collected all the acts of ingratitude of the *dēmos* towards its generals. Plutarch thus recognises an anti-democratic bias in many of his authorities. This is interesting; he is himself no supporter of 'democracy', in this or any other context.

Scholarly discussion of this kind, even though it only comes to light occasionally in the *Lives*, was presumably the common stuff of Plutarch's historical thinking. Intrinsic probability, external evidence, and the known credit of the source all come into his arguments. His 'probability' (*eikos*) includes considerations which we should regard as dubious and subjective; and there are other ways too in which his criteria are unfamiliar and unconvincing.

His attitude to chronological data is a case in point. There was a famous story, told by Herodotus, that Solon visited King Croesus of Lydia. As Croesus came to the throne nearly thirty-five years after Solon's archonship, the story conflicts with the accepted chronology of the period, and Plutarch knew it did. Yet:

I do not think I can abandon a story so famous, attested by so many

[30] The 'trial' did indeed become a subject for rhetorical exercises (*Prolegomena in Staseis*, p. 208 Rabe).

witnesses, and—most important—so appropriate to Solon's character and worthy of his greatness of soul and wisdom, because of what are called 'canons of chronology', which countless authors have tried to get right, without so far succeeding in reducing their discrepancies to a consistent account. (*Solon* 27)

This is not, as is sometimes thought, a frivolous excuse for not rejecting a story which Plutarch knows in his heart to be false. He believes it. The judgment he is making is that the statements of the chronographers—Eratosthenes or Apollodorus or some successor—are less reliable than the premiss that Solon's known character makes the story probable. It is not an unreasonable position.

Again,[31] there was a discrepancy between the authorities as to which Persian king was on the throne when the exiled Themistocles arrived at the court. Thucydides and Charon of Lampsacus said it was Artaxerxes: 'Ephorus, Dinon, Clitarchus, Heraclides and others' that it was Xerxes himself. Plutarch observes that Thucydides is in closer accord with the chronological tables, though they are themselves far from secure. This is in fact the most vexed chronological crux of the period between the Persian and Peloponnesian Wars.[32] Plutarch does not discuss it in any detail, and we have to guess the lines on which he is thinking. They are perhaps these: (*i*) chronological tables are unreliable; (*ii*) it is however a point in Thucydides' favour that he can be more easily reconciled with them; (*iii*) anyway, Thucydides is a very reliable man.[33] He therefore accepts the version in which the king is Artaxerxes. Consequently, in the narrative that follows he is unable to make rhetorical use of the confrontation between two old enemies which the other story implies. A certain reluctance shows through: he avoids the king's name altogether. Where Plutarch's feeling differs from that which is instinctive to the modern critic is, I think, that it does not occur to him that the

---

[31] *Themistocles* 27.

[32] For a general discussion, see A. W. Gomme, *Thucydides I*, 398 ff.

[33] cf. (e.g.) 25. In 855B–C, Plutarch draws attention to Thucydides' lack of malice in writing about Cleon, Hyperbolus and Nicias. His milder language makes him a more credible witness.

version in Ephorus and the other later writers is *ben trovato*. He is not conditioned to think that the rhetorically effective is likely to be an invention, just as in the story of Solon and Croesus he is not conditioned to regard a morally improving anecdote as likely to be fictitious; in that case, indeed, the moral aspect is a recommendation to believe.

It is, then, Thucydides' own credit, gained by the impression he makes elsewhere, that tips the scale in his favour. It is not the fact that he is an earlier writer or nearer the events. Plutarch in fact has special reservations about contemporary writers. A little earlier in *Themistocles* (25), he reports a statement of the fifth-century rhapsode and pamphleteer Stesimbrotus to the effect that Themistocles sailed to Sicily and asked the tyrant Hieron for his daughter in marriage, promising in return to subdue Greece to his power. The refutation of this is not here made to rest on the intrinsic unreliability of Stesimbrotus, though it is clear enough what Plutarch thought of him. Two other arguments are adduced: (*i*) the story is not probable (*eikos*) because Theophrastus tells us that Themistocles exhorted the crowd to tear down the tyrant's tents at Olympia; (*ii*) it is in contradiction with the narrative in Thucydides. But in another place,[34] Plutarch rejects a scandalous story reported by Stesimbrotus about Pericles and his daughter-in-law. And here he comments:

So difficult is truth, so hard for history to track down! Those who come later find that time obstructs their knowledge of events, whereas history that is contemporary with actions and personalities mars and perverts truth either by jealousy and malice or by flattery and favour.

In other words, a contemporary author is particularly liable to *ira et studium*, and the researcher must be specially on his guard. What is disconcerting in the case of Stesimbrotus is to find Plutarch using so obviously second-hand a source as Theophrastus, and a dubious anecdote at that, to refute the slander which he finds objectionable.

[34] *Pericles* 13.15.

What we think of as tendentiousness in history, Plutarch tends to think of as malice: a more emotional, subjective and rhetorical way of looking at it. Many of the great historians, in his view, indulged this failing. Certainly Theopompus did. No one else knew that the Thebans accepted Spartan money to induce them to withdraw from Laconia in 370, yet 'somehow or other' Theopompus got wind of it.[35] And Plutarch was clearly aware that the tendency of the digression on Athenian demagogues in *Philippica* $\bar{X}$ led to serious misjudgments. How, he asks,[36] could Demosthenes be accused of being 'unstable in character, unable to stay long with the same policy or the same people'? He did in fact not only hold consistently to the same line of policy, but he sacrificed his life for it. Later writers like Douris, who combined prejudice with a taste for the melodramatic, are even more severely criticised. Douris could not even keep his narrative to the truth when his own feelings were not directly involved.[37]

The sharpest attack is reserved for Herodotus. This is not in the *Lives*; if that was all we had, we should remark merely on the comparative rarity of reference and on the fact that Plutarch does not use Herodotus as much as we might have expected for the Persian Wars. We should doubt whether he knew him very well. It is another book, *Herodotus' Malice* (854E), that proves that in fact he knew him intimately.

This is a puzzling little work. It reads as a more pungent and one-sided version of the kind of discussion we have been considering. Perhaps it could be called a kind of scholarly *controversia*. Herodotus is, as it were, on trial in the imagination, and any forensic cliché or sharp practice can be used to discredit him. The main complaint is in effect his failure to conceal the pro-Persian sympathies of the Boeotians. This is an example of his general malevolence. A single instance will show the tone. In describing the fighting at Sigeum, Herodotus (5.95) said nothing of the brave deeds of Pittacus, but a good deal about the cowardice of the poet Alcaeus. 'By not recording good deeds and not omit-

[35] *Agesilaus* 32–3.   [36] *Demosthenes* 13.
[37] *Pericles* 28; cf. *Eumenes* 1, *Alcibiades* 32 (on this, see below, p. 126).

ting bad, he confirms the view that jealousy and gloating over misfortune (*epichairekakia*) spring from the same vice.' Writing history is an extension of our everyday activity of conversation and social life; the same ethical principles apply. This of course is for Plutarch a serious point; there is nothing in *Herodotus' Malice*, however ingenious and implausible the techniques of declamation, that does not accord with the principles that he believed to govern social and intellectual life. The most instructive part of the book is the introduction, in which Plutarch enumerates the ways in which a historian may display 'malice'. There is no forced ingenuity here; only a clear statement of the diagnostic signs. There are eight of them. (*i*) He uses needlessly pejorative terms; (*ii*) he inserts discreditable facts when they are not relevant and leaves out creditable considerations even when they are; (*iii*) he damns with faint praise; (*iv*) when there are two alternative accounts, he chooses the less creditable; and (*v*) when various motives are possible he assigns the less respectable. He has subtler tricks besides. He disparages achievements by attributing them to luck or minimising their intrinsic difficulty (*vi*). He will denounce a discreditable version—but record it all the same (*vii*). He mixes praise and blame so fiendishly as to cast doubt even on the praise (*viii*).

These are, looked at from the other side, recognised rhetorical techniques of innuendo and disparagement. They do indeed play a part in ancient historiography; Plutarch's contemporary Tacitus is a great master in their use. To point out their presence in an adversary is a way of discrediting him in turn. This however is not the whole of what Plutarch is doing here. His own attitudes, and still more his practice as a biographer, make it clear that we should take him as expressing something genuinely important to him and implying a writer's code of conduct. In the controversies and *problēmata* which he includes in the *Lives*, it is often the 'malicious' tendency, in this sense, that he opposes and refutes. In his own choice of variants, he would rather be on the side of generosity of interpretation. This is how the good man ought to write history. In his own words:

Since it is difficult, or rather perhaps impossible, to display a man's life as pure and blameless, we should fill out the truth to give a likeness where the good points lie, but regard the errors and follies with which emotion or political necessity sullies a career as deficiencies in some virtue rather than displays of viciousness, and therefore not make any special effort to draw attention to them in the record. Our attitude should be one of modest shame on behalf of human nature, which never produces unmixed good or a character of undisputed excellence.[83]

Our brief look at Plutarch's learning and its uses and methods may appropriately rest here. His style, even more than his scholarly apparatus, reveals his vast and catholic reading. In the scales of his honest criticism, the truths of morality weigh very heavy; probability and consistency are important criteria, and he often seems to give less than due weight to what appears to be the crucial fact. He is moreover, like most ancient historians, a trained rhetorician, and perhaps subtler than he is sometimes thought. He would claim to put this skill also at the service of morality. In his own fashion, he is *vir bonus dicendi peritus*. Consistent attitudes and methods run right through his work. We have seen them in relation to poetry and history; we shall see them also when we look at the professed work of his life, his philosophy.

[38] *Cimon* 2. 4–5.

CHAPTER FOUR

The Philosopher and his Religion

PLUTARCH was a declared and consistent Platonist, even if he was not in all respects in agreement with the orthodoxy of the school.

In his youth, the Stoics were the leading sect, the allegiance one would think of first when a man described himself as a philosopher. It was the age of Seneca, Epictetus and the influential group of first-century Roman Stoics. By the end of Plutarch's life, however, the picture, seen in these very simple colours, had changed. The philosopher *par excellence* was now a *Platonicus*. Stoicism still had its great exponents, even a Marcus Aurelius; but in the second and third centuries, new and developing forms of Platonism came to overshadow every other adherence. Where there was open conflict and open compromise between Christian thinkers and their pagan opponents, it was with the Platonists. No one else mattered.

The reasons for this movement towards Platonism are complex and not clearly known. But there is one comparatively superficial factor which needs to be stressed. Plato, alone among the founders of schools, was a literary classic. Aristotle's 'golden fluency',[1] though admired, made a thin claim compared with his master's treasures of pure Attic. This was an important point in an age which consciously looked to a rather remote past, and saw it mainly through the medium of its literary patrimony. Not that the Atticists admired Plato's style without reservation. There was

[1] Cicero, *Academica* 2.119.

a strong tradition of disapproval of its more poetic and 'dithy-rambic' features. Dionysius complained of the hocus-pocus in Plato's grand style; 'Longinus', with his more baroque taste, defended precisely the grandeur and metaphorical richness. In any case, however, Plato was a storehouse of the older language, and his text invited interpretation from grammarian and philosopher alike.

And certainly philosophy, as Plutarch knew it, was a scholarly business, much concerned with the interpretation of texts. Here, as in history, there were *problēmata* and differences between authorities to be reconciled. The classical philosophers, like the classical poets, did not always mean what they seemed on the surface to say. In handling all this, Plutarch shows once again the verbal sophistication in argument, the reliance on *eikos*, the certainty about moral principles, which his work in other fields reveals. With Plato, as with Hesiod or Herodotus, his scholar-ship sometimes disconcerts by its aridity and apparent frivolity. What for instance are we to make of the 'Platonic' interpreta-tion of the Delphic E? Plutarch is speaking[2] in the dialogue *The Delphic 'E'* in his own person, even though he does represent himself as a young man; he is working out the consequences of believing the mysterious E to be the numeral five, and he naturally draws on the sort of number-symbolism that we asso-ciate mainly with the Pythagoreans. He goes on to find fives in Plato: the 'first principles' of *Sophist* 256C, Being, The Same, The Other, Movement, Rest; the four principles of *Philebus* 23C, Infinite, Finite, Becoming, Cause of Combination—made up to five by adding Cause of Dissolution; the five categories of the Good in *Philebus* 66A. There have been ages in which this kind of interpretation of a religious symbol would have been taken in earnest; but it can hardly be so with Plutarch, and his accumu-lation of alternatives perhaps itself gives the clue. This is mock-metaphysics, or at most an ambivalent game between earnest and parody. One thinks not only of Plato but of Sir Thomas Browne's quincunxes and the Cambridge Platonists.

[2] 391A; cf. 428B.

However, the tone of Plutarch's more important pieces of Platonic interpretation is grave enough, and they have a serious bearing on his deeper convictions. The most substantial extant piece is the lengthy discussion (1012A) of the account Plato gives in *Timaeus* 35A of the creation of the 'world-soul'. This is complicated and mathematical; but it touches some central points in Plutarch's thinking. He held the unusual view, shared notably by Atticus, an influential Platonist of the later second century who may derive it from Plutarch himself, that Plato meant the creation of the kosmos in the *Timaeus* literally. The world really was created in time, and the story of its making was not, as most Platonists held, a symbolic analysis of an eternally-existing order. Plutarch's ostensible reason for believing this is the scholarly one of making Plato self-consistent (1013E). He complains of his predecessors that they are more concerned to make the philosopher say acceptable things than to reconcile him with himself. Without creation in time, he thinks, the 'priority' or 'seniority' of the soul, and its activity as the initiator of change and movement, on which Plato insists elsewhere, would be empty of meaning. In his own view, what existed before the kosmos was *akosmia*, 'disorder', and this involved both body or matter (*sōma*) and mind or soul (*psuchē*). The *psuchē* which was responsible for movement in the *akosmia* was disordered and did not possess reason. Now Plato spoke of a *psuchē* which was disordered and productive of evil also in the *Laws* (896D), and Plutarch equates this with the disordered *psuchē* of the pre-cosmic confusion. To this and not to matter is to be assigned the cause of evil in the world. Plato, he argues (1014F), could not have regarded matter as the cause of evil and also spoken of it[3] as without quality and comparable to the odourless oils which perfumers use as the base of their products.

This intricate interpretation has features very typical of ancient philosophical schools. Emphasis on the self-consistency of one's own view and the self-contradictions of others is one such feature; it is a natural consequence of the polemical study of texts. Typical

[3] *Timaeus* 50E.

too is the report of earlier opinions, *doxai*, with which Plutarch begins. This a regular feature in philosophical writing from Aristotle onwards. Plutarch gives us another good example of it in the opening chapters of *Moral Virtue*, and one of the great extant collections of *doxai* is preserved in the corpus of his works, though it shows no internal evidence of being his doing, and its connection with him must remain uncertain.

But the significance of the *Timaeus* commentary goes beyond that of scholastic debate. The interpretation Plutarch seeks is not just one that holds water and satisfies the texts, but one which will accord with his own convictions about the good and evil in the world. He seems always to have kept in mind, as something of central importance, the belief that disorder and evil are of psychic, not material origin. There are, for him, 'evil souls' at work, and our ability to change the world or ourselves for better is limited by their existence and depends on our recognition of it. He worried about these problems all his life.

Now allegiance to Plato implied a certain measure of hostility to other sects. Of course, philosophers generally agreed against the outside world, especially in matters of morals; but the basic differences of principle between the sects were real enough, and amply sufficed to create and perpetuate rivalries and dislike, in somewhat the same way as sectarian differences in Christianity. That there was not much bloodshed among philosophers is presumably due to the fact that these things were the preoccupation of a minority who did not often succeed in inflaming the mob. 'Christians out! Epicureans out!' shouts the hostile crowd in Lucian's *Alexander* (38). Plutarch is not likely to have heard this sinister noise; it belongs to the world of mass-movements which he viewed from a distance.

Even in Plutarch, however, polemic sometimes descends to personalities. When an Epicurean appears in a dialogue (548A), it is to vanish in a huff and leave his hearers staring. The eccentric Cynic Didymus in *The Decline of Oracles* is a comic figure (413A). He strikes the ground with his stick, opines that the oracle ought to have packed up long ago because of the silly questions people ask, and finally goes off in dudgeon without speaking. It is of course difficult to measure dislike. In all ancient literature we have to do with a pervasive tradition of exaggerated invective, which spread from litigation and politics into the world of learning and science. It is tempting to put down all Plutarch's fulminations and innuendos as meaningless convention.

But it would be wrong, just as it would be wrong to regard *Herodotus' Malice* as a mere exercise by an author uncommitted to any underlying principle. Plutarch is in earnest. Not only did he think of Stoics and Epicureans as professional rivals, proper objects for the rudeness of controversy; he regarded them as fundamentally wrong, and their teaching as pernicious. And this indignation sprang from the integrated set of religious and moral convictions which he held.

Epicureanism had had a great history. A century or so earlier, it had passed through a phase when it was both fashionable and influential in the Roman world: the age of Lucretius and Caesar. The receding tide left a collection of moral topics on which even opponents drew freely. The *Moral Letters* of the Stoic Seneca were to some extent modelled on Epicurus', whose *gnōmai* he often quotes. In *Superstition* (164E) Plutarch repeatedly reminds us of Lucretius; they had a common inspiration in Epicurean writing. Nevertheless, the refutation of the atomism and the hedonism was for Plutarch in the main a standard academic exercise. It had a pedagogic function. The arguments were well established, the young student could master them and improve them in detail as he would an anecdote or a comparison at his rhetor's school, and he was stimulated by the thought that he was breaking a lance in defence of the approved values of religion and morality.

Three of Plutarch's anti-Epicurean works survive. Four or five other titles are known. One of the extant pieces (1128), a declamation making play with Epicurus' advice to 'live unnoticed', shows how a philosophical topic can be handled with a purely rhetorical technique. The other two are more substantial. Both take their subject from a book by an immediate disciple of

Epicurus, Colotes, who had argued that the doctrines of all non-Epicureans 'make even life impossible'—i.e. not only are they fallacious but they prevent the ordinary activities of humanity. The first of Plutarch's answers (1107D) to this three-centuries-old charge consists of a review of the interpretations of philosophers that Colotes gave; it is an informative and eloquent book. Its companion-piece (1086c), formally a dialogue but virtually a monologue spoken by Theon, turns the tables on the Epicureans by arguing that their precepts, quite apart from their other weaknesses, do not 'even' allow us a 'pleasant' life—which of course Epicurus and his followers regarded as the whole and only good.

There are also anti-Stoic writings, and at first sight they present a strikingly similar picture:[4] three extant polemics (1033A–1086B), the titles of six more. Of the surviving works, one is a treatise, one a declamation, one a very undramatic dialogue on 'common notions'. The declamation takes the theme that Stoic paradoxes are stranger than the poets' fictions. The treatise pertinaciously hunts contradictions in the texts of a philosophy which, after all, made much of 'living consistently'. It was evidently the companion-piece of the lost *Contradictions of the Epicureans*; we observe again how large a part attack on, and defence of, apparent inconsistencies played in all these scholastic debates.

The Stoics, however, were much more worthwhile and serious adversaries in Plutarch's eyes than the Epicureans. Not only these formal polemics, but certain other works are directed against their views. *Moral Virtue* (440D) and *Progress in Virtue* (75A) are the most notable of these, but the books on animal psychology —*The Intelligence of Animals* (959A) and *Gryllus* (985D)—are also by implication anti-Stoic, since Plutarch held that animals also had *logos* and man was not unique in this: a theme related to the vegetarianism to which he seems to have been attracted.[5] More than this, the anti-Stoic tone is often recognisable where any topic occurs to which it might be relevant. It is modified only by admiration for Stoic achievements and heroism, as in the encom-

---

[4] See in general D. Babut, *Plutarque et le stoïcisme*, Paris 1969.
[5] See especially the two speeches on meat-eating, 993A–999B.

iastic life of the younger Cato, where Plutarch enters into the spirit of the extremely laudatory narratives that he follows. The debate between the Academy and the Stoa took shape in the third century B.C., and these old controversies still provide the fuel for Plutarch's arguments; but the reason why the fire burned so brightly lies, once again, in its relevance to his own general convictions. He sees in Stoicism something fundamentally hostile to his ethical belief in the value of kindness and humanity, and to that sense of human frailty and cosmic imperfection in which he reminds us of the classic attitudes of early Greece, the modest confidence and tempered pessimism of a Herodotus or a Sophocles.

Plutarch was thus a traditionalist in his philosophy, as in much else; an expert in the debates of the schools; a convinced Platonist; and a serious person who had no intention of putting his life and his theories into separate compartments. At least, this is the *persona*; wherever we look in his works, it is maintained with remarkable consistency. We should perhaps allow ourselves to believe that it is the man himself.

The centre of gravity of Plutarch's philosophy lay in ethics. Physical science and theology subserved moral ends, as they usually do in Hellenistic thought. But he did not neglect them. Neither did Seneca, who wrote his elaborate *Natural Questions* at a time when he was also delving deeply into moral theory and problems.

The moral orientation of Plutarch's science is well seen in the elaborate and famous dialogue, *The Face in the Moon*.[6]

The setting is curious. Lamprias, Plutarch's brother, relates a conversation with some friends in which he and one Lucius, a pupil of the well-known Pythagorean Moderatus of Gades, report an earlier discussion in their circle about the nature of the moon. They do this, apparently, in order to give Sextius Sulla a chance to tell an extraordinary story he has picked up from a

[6] H. Cherniss gives an excellent edition in the Loeb *Moralia*, vol. XII; see also S. Sambursky, *The Physical World of the Greeks*, 204 ff.

traveller recently returned to Carthage from an adventure in the Atlantic. The beginning of the dialogue is missing, but the essential point about Sulla's promised myth is clear. Ostensibly, the subject is to be the 'face' seen in the moon. In fact, the first part of the book is an application of arguments from physics and optics not only to this point but to general questions about the moon's nature. Peripatetic and Stoic theories are expounded. Clearchus' idea that the 'face' is a reflection of the terrestrial Ocean is praised as showing his boldness and elegance. The main effort is once again directed against the Stoics. Their representative is Pharnaces: unknown, not very clearly characterised and treated as something of a butt, but not necessarily a figment. The Stoics held that the moon was composed of air and fire; Plutarch, as a Platonist, that its substance is earth. He sets out to show that the Stoics are not consistent with themselves. The fire they posit could not exist without solid material (922A). Certain humorous allegorists indeed saw this, he tells us, when they made Hephaestus' lameness and inability to walk without a wooden stick a symbol of the inability of fire to gain ground without fuel. Plutarch's 'humorists' are clearly Stoic, and their humour unintentional. Indeed, the extant first-century Stoic allegorists, Cornutus and 'Heraclitus', both report the interpretation— Cornutus (18) in similar words (*probainein* for 'walk'). Again (922, 930), the Stoics held that light alters air from dark to light in an instant, as we see at the sunrise; why then is the moon not evenly illuminated all over? Its shadows, and indeed its phases, become inexplicable. Moreover (933D), if it is air and fire, surely it should be invisible when it shines against the bright background of the surrounding *aither*, not, as it is, when it is darkened and eclipsed. Worst of all (925 ff.), the Stoics held the doctrine of 'natural place', according to which the elements tend to a particular level, with earth at rest in the centre. This leads them into various difficulties. The universe cannot be infinite, for then it would have no centre. The Stoic fire-soul and pantheist immanent God would be impossible; they would be fire in the wrong places. There would be no use for providence either, for the places of the elements would be determined—whereas in fact Stoicism lays great stress on providence and teleology, and on things being in the 'best' place, not only in the human body but in the *kosmos* itself, seen as a vast organism. 'Everywhere, the principle of the greater good is more important than that of necessity' (928C). The debating points are shrewd. Plutarch deploys his knowledge of physics and optics efficiently to make his case. But it all remains in the familiar vein of controversial scoring—at least until the play with paradoxes passes over into the talk of providence and teleology, and the larger issues bring with them the warmer style of moral concern and protreptic.

Lamprias' speech (934A ff.), however, develops a more positive view of the phenomena. In the course of it, we find him (934C ff.) drawing attention to the different colours visible during a lunar eclipse—something which also interested the astrologers—and coming to the conclusion that the dark, earthy colour is the moon's own, while the rest are due to the light all round her. There follows a passage of characteristic fantasy:

Seeing that here on earth places shaded by purple and red awnings take up colour from them and glow with it, when they are next to pools or rivers open to the sun, giving off many different radiations because of the reflections, is it to be wondered at if a huge stream of shadow pouring into a heavenly ocean, as it were, of moving, restless light, shot through by innumerable stars and receiving all kinds of combinations and changes of colour, should soak up various tints from the moon and reproduce them here? A star or a fire would not appear grey or dark blue in shadow, whereas over mountains, plains and seas there flit many kinds of colours from the sun, and its brilliance induces in the shadows and mists with which it mingles tints like those produced in a painter's colours. Homer has endeavoured to give a name somehow to the tints of the sea: he speaks of 'wine-dark deep', 'purple wave', 'grey sea', 'white calm'. But he neglects—as being infinite in number—the diversities of constantly changing colours that are found on the earth. Now the moon, in all probability, does not have a single plane surface like the sea, but resembles in its structure the earth that old Socrates described in his myth—whether he meant our earth by his enigmatic description or some other. There is nothing incredible or extraordinary in the notion that the moon, who has nothing corrupt or sordid in her, but gathers pure light from heaven and is full of a heat that is not burning nor furious but liquid, innocuous and natural, may possess marvellously beautiful places, flaming mountains, zones of purple, gold and silver not scattered sparsely in her depths but breaking out in abundance on her plains and visible on her smooth uplands. (934D–935A)

This kind of description, in which Plutarch strains language to convey marvellous effects of light and colour, recurs in two of the great 'underworld myths' which he composed on Platonic models (563B ff., 589F ff.). The idea of the wonderful lights is part of the imaginative legacy of astronomy, easily carried over to the language of religious vision. But the special care for colour seems peculiar to Plutarch, who evidently had an eye for it and an interest in the problem of expressing it verbally. The reference to Homer is striking; here is another scrap of commentator's learning serving a new purpose.

But it is not only the colour that makes Lamprias' moon so strange. Imagination is leaving scientific theory behind. The 'probability' (*eikos*) about the moon's nature comes from the myth of Plato's *Phaedo*, which describes the splendours of the 'true earth', evidently a symbol of the world of 'forms'. Plutarch builds on the imagery of that grandiose vision. He interprets it as *possibly* a parable of the moon; but Lamprias is a good Academic, and cannot be dogmatic about it.

The passage from science to fantasy should not be misinterpreted. It is to miss the tone and purpose of the dialogue to detect a clash between the clarity and acumen of the preceding arguments on astrophysics and the moon-mythology that begins hereabouts. Both science and religious myth belong to the same range of elevated 'cosmic' subjects. They demand elaboration and magnificence, not bare factual statement. Plato set the pattern in the *Timaeus*. Plutarch's knowledge of Hellenistic science enlarged the material for his metaphysical and moralising fantasy, it did not give him the objective tone of the modern physicist.

And as we read on, the mythical predominates more and more.

Is the moon inhabited? Theon suggests that moon-men would fall off, be burnt up, have no nourishment. Lamprias replies in detail. It is no proof, he says, to say that an uninhabited moon would serve no purpose in the universe. After all, parts of the earth are desert. But in fact the moon may have inhabitants; the smooth rotation would hold them on, there may be plants and trees that need no rain or snow, she may have cooling and softening qualities herself. If there are living creatures on her, we cannot indeed imagine them—but this does not mean they do not exist. Here come more Platonic touches:

Indeed, they may be much more amazed at the earth, when they see that sediment and muddy residue of the universe appearing amid its damps and mists and clouds, a low, unlit, unmoving spot. Can it, they may wonder, really produce and nourish living things possessed of movement, respiration and warmth? (940E)

Sulla too is concerned with the inhabitants of the moon. His story, long awaited, proves indeed a remarkable one, in which Plutarch has woven together several traditional themes. One is the myth of the imprisonment of Kronos on a distant island in the far west. There are echoes here of Plato's Atlantis, but also of other tales that grew up in the period when Britain and the remoter west of Europe were a favoured setting for utopian romance.[7] Another common motif of fantasy, the discovery of sacred books, is also alluded to, but not used in a way at all integral to the story.[8] Essentially, the tale is one of personal revelation: the 'servants of Kronos' disclose religious truths to the traveller.

What they tell symbolises an elaborate psychological doctrine. Body, *psuchē* and *nous* (intelligence) are three separate things, even more distinct than the three 'parts' of Plato's *psuchē*. There are two deaths: one, the separation of body from the rest, which takes place on earth; the other, the separation of *nous* from *psuchē*,

[7] e.g. the first-century novel of Antonius Diogenes, *Wonders Beyond Thule*, known from Photius, cod. 166.

[8] On this, see W. Speyer, *Bücherfunde in der Glaubenswerbung der Antike*, Göttingen 1970.

which takes place on the moon after a lengthy period of puri-
fication and awaiting. For as the soul ascends after its first death,
it wanders and undergoes punishment in the atmosphere between
earth and moon. The length of time it spends here, in 'the mea-
dows of Hades', depends on its moral condition. Arrival on the
moon brings joy, fright, hope: a bewildering excitement like that
of initiation into the mysteries. The moon is therefore inhabited
by beings who have got thus far; these are *daimones*, and they are
still liable to suffer for wrongs done and to be sent down to earth
to look after oracles, punish wrongdoers, and protect men in
battle or at sea. One day, however, 'love for the image of the sun'
may procure their further release; *nous* then escapes from *psuchē*,
who then stays dreaming on the moon until she is ultimately
accepted and assimilated by her, as the body is by earth. There is a
reverse process too: the sun 'sows' *nous* on the moon, and she
forms *psuchai* with it; these pass to earth and there receive bodies.
The moon therefore is the only part of the universe that both
receives and takes; she is the essential middle stage in the whole
process of generation. As in the *Republic*, it is the Moirai—the
Fates—who preside over the whole affair. Atropos, on the sun,
sets the process going; Clotho, moving round on the moon,
'binds and combines'; Lachesis, the chanciest of the three, joins
in as the souls approach earth.

The elements of this fantasy come from many places. They
include Platonic reminiscences, traces of astrology, much literary
as well as popular tradition. The synthesis is Plutarch's; he did
not find the scheme as it is in earlier writers. Later, as it seems, in
Socrates' Sign (591B), he made another construction out of much
the same pieces.[9] There however it is a metaphysical, not a
psychological, scheme in which the sun and the moon play their
part and the three Moirai hold the keys.

The history of literary visions of the underworld runs from
Homer to Dante and beyond. Plutarch holds an important place

[9] The relative dating is, I think, assured by the comparison between the two
schemes, since it is actually difficult to understand the scheme in *Socrates' Sign*
without knowledge of the other.

in the story. He lavished art and ingenuity on these elaborate set-pieces, in which imitation of Plato did not prevent him from adumbrating doctrines Plato never knew and creating fantasies in the taste of his own age.

So the inhabitants of the moon are *daimones*. What does this signify? In *The Decline of Oracles* (410B), a certain Cleombrotus of Sparta is made to tell some strange stories. He was a great traveller, and the object of his travels was 'to gather information (*historia*) as the raw material, as it were, of a philosophy which, to use his own words, made theology (*theologia*) its ultimate aim.' Cleombrotus is perhaps not to be taken too seriously; there is a distinct difference between his activity and what we may suppose to have been Plutarch's, for whom *theologia*, as for Plato, is bound by patterns of morality. Exotic wisdom, however fascinating, needed, in Plutarch's view, critical sifting. It follows that when Cleombrotus says that the doctrine of *daimones*, in the sense of beings supposed to be intermediate between gods and men, has been of greater value in philosophy than Plato's doctrine of 'matter', he may well be showing more enthusiasm than Plutarch himself felt. But that this concept, or rather group of concepts, is important to Plutarch is plain, not only from the set expositions here and in *Isis and Osiris*, but from its incidental use in psychology, in the interpretation of myth, and in the *Lives*.

In *Isis and Osiris*,[10] Plutarch seeks an acceptable explanation of the appalling story of Osiris' treacherous murder and subsequent dismemberment by Typhon. He distinguishes such tales from mere poetic fiction: this is a significant myth, Egyptian tradition is ancient and important. A historical or 'Euhemeristic' interpretation is impious and will not do. 'Better'—less offensive, more appropriate—is the approach suggested by the doctrine of *daimones*. This has its classic authorities: Pythagoras, Plato, Plato's pupil Xenocrates, the Stoic Chrysippus, all basing themselves on earlier *theologoi*. In the parallel account in Cleombrotus'

[10] See especially 358E–361E.

speech (414F), Zoroaster and other foreign sources are mentioned as well, no doubt in keeping with Cleombrotus' exotic interests and experiences. And in both accounts there are poetical as well as philosophical *auctores*. Thus, in *Isis* we are told how Homer used the adjective *daimonios* of good and bad alike, so anticipating the view of Xenocrates and others that some *daimones* have sinister natures. Cleombrotus in turn adduces slightly different pieces of scholarly information: that Homer uses *daimones* as a synonym of *theoi* (gods), and that Hesiod[11] was the first to distinguish clearly the various grades of rational being: gods, *daimones*, heroes, men. It was indeed this passage of Hesiod, together with the statements about *daimones* in Plato's *Symposium*, that formed the central justificatory texts which later writers on these subjects were in the habit of adducing.[12] Cleombrotus' account however goes further; he takes up the bizarre analogy which Xenocrates[13] made between *daimones* and isosceles triangles, which are neither equilateral nor scalene but between the two, partaking of the nature of both. He also adopts the idea, which we have already encountered, of some association between *daimones* and the moon, the moon being the intermediary in the system of the universe. Finally, he attributes sinister and cruel actions to some *daimones*. How seriously Plutarch took all this is hard to say. Of course he makes use of the ideas elsewhere, and notably in the myths; but his final attitude may be rather one of Academic reserve than of commitment. We must not forget that Cleombrotus' arguments are not left untouched in the subsequent discussion, and the concluding speech of Lamprias leaves the *daimones* with only a minor role in the explanation of the prophetic power of the oracle.

We saw that, as an interpreter of Plato, Plutarch viewed the cause of evil in the world as psychical and not material. No doubt he was tempted to link this doctrine with the concept of demonic

---

[11] *Works and Days* 122.
[12] G. Soury, *La Démonologie de Plutarque*, is the most substantial treatment of all this, though he represents Plutarch's views as more coherent than they probably were.
[13] R. Heinze, *Xenokrates*, 79.

beings, whether disembodied souls or demigods, some of whom might be dangerously spiteful and malicious unless their anger was turned by apotropaic rituals. This seems to have been what Xenocrates held. It is not clear whether Plutarch finally formed a view about it, but he certainly knew and reflected on the possibility. No doubt also he shared a religious sentiment characteristic of the age: the demand for mediators between god and man. This is a widespread phenomenon of the age when Christianity took root; perhaps we may plausibly see it as a natural consequence, in an anxious population, of the distancing of the divine from ordinary experience that followed from the Hellenistic diffusion of philosophical ideas. The word *daimon* had a long and confused history. Originally 'allotter', it naturally came to mean luck, and hence the destiny or, more personally, the 'guardian angel' of an individual. This concept has no necessary connection either with that of the intermediary or with that of the active but disembodied soul. But the connection is often made in practice. Plutarch relates 'guardian' to 'mediator' most explicitly in *Socrates' Sign*, at least if we are meant to interpret the myth, with its *nous-daimon*, in terms of Theanor's account of the divine guidance of Epaminondas. Sometimes he is more cautious; in this connection it is worth looking at his handling of one of the most famous supernatural stories in the tradition, the appearance of the phantom to Brutus in Asia[14]

It was a dark night, and the light in the tent was not very bright. The whole camp was still. Brutus was thinking about something and turning it over in his mind, when he became aware of someone coming in. Looking towards the door, he saw a weird and terrible vision . . . 'Who are you?' he cried, 'god or man? Why have you come to me?' 'I am your evil *daimon*, Brutus,' answered the phantom; 'you will see me at Philippi.' 'I will,' answered Brutus, unperturbed . . . In the morning he went to Cassius and told him of the vision. Now Cassius was an Epicurean . . . 'Our view, Brutus,' he said, 'is that not all our experiences or visions are true; perception is malleable and deceptive, and the mind

[14] *Brutus* 36 ff.: F. E. Brenk, in *Actes du VIII* *Congrès* . . . *Budé*, 1969, 588 ff.

is even quicker than the senses to shift and change to any kind of thing with no factual cause. Wax is moulded from without; the human mind, which comprises within itself both the moulder and the moulded, can easily shape and vary itself by its own devices. Witness the sudden turns that our imaginative faculty takes in dreams, when it moves in response to all kinds of experiences and images from a slight cause; its nature is to be in perpetual motion, and the motion is an act of imagining or thinking. In your case, a fatigued body naturally produces an oscillation and distortion of the mind. As to *daimones*: it is not likely they exist, and if they do it is not likely they should have human shape or voice or power that can penetrate to us. I wish they had, so that we, as champions of piety and honour, might have had divine help to give us confidence, and not only arms and horses and ships.'

The strange thing about this passage is that the Epicurean Cassius' explanation could hardly be less Epicurean in content. Epicurus held that the senses were veracious, not that they were unreliable, and that gods at least were seen by men in dreams in human form. It would have been easy to construct an Epicurean view of a harmless atomic phantom. But Plutarch has not done this; he has given us the speech of an unbeliever, but in Aristotelian or Academic terms. It is tempting to think that this is Plutarch's kind of scepticism in the face of a story of this sort. At any rate there is nothing here to suggest the intermediary or guardian *daimon*.

It must, I think, be wrong to attribute any firm system of 'demonology' to Plutarch. Literary and philosophical tradition, the wisdom of the East, the popular beliefs of Hellas, were all known to him. They provided material for conjecture and adaptation. If he ever came to a definite approval or rejection, it was on the ground of moral 'probabilities'.

Nor is this true only of *daimones*. More fundamental religious issues, immortality and the validity of cult, make the same sort of impression. Even in the *Consolation* to his wife on the death of the child Timoxena (608A), there is a curious hesitancy. Belief in immortality is there all right, but it is restrained and uncertain. 'It is harder to disbelieve than to believe in' our departure to a better place: a truly Academic absence of dogma. The emphasis in the *Consolation* lies rather on the warning repeatedly given against ostentatious emotionalism in mourning. Plutarch seems particularly anxious lest his wife should disgrace herself—and him— by some feminine indulgence in superstitious practice. Exhortation rather than comfort is the dominant note. And this concern with outward behaviour and propriety in religion recurs in many places. Decency seems almost more central to Plutarch's religion than belief.

Superstition (164E) is a key text. It is a rather declamatory piece, in which superstition (*deisidaimonia*) is made out to be a worse evil than the opposite extreme of atheism. It is represented as the most abject kind of terror:

He who fears god fears everything—earth, sea, air, heaven, darkness, light, sound, silence, dreams. Slaves forget their masters in sleep, sleep lightens prisoners' chains; inflamed wounds, savage ulcers of the flesh, excruciating pains, all cease when the patient rests:

O dear consoling sleep, help in my sickness,
how sweet your coming to me in my need![15]

Superstition does not let you say this. She alone makes no truce with sleep but denies the mind this unique chance of achieving relaxation and renewed confidence by repulsing her bitter and painful doctrines concerning the divine. The sleep of the superstitious is like the Hell of the wicked: superstition rouses fearsome images of demons, monstrous phantoms, avenging Furies. She torments the wretched soul, she chases it from sleep with nightmares. Flogged and beaten at its own hands, the soul imagines it suffers at the hands of others and accepts bizarre and terrible commands. (165D ff.)

Death itself brings no relief:

Hell's 'deep gates' open, rivers of fire coalesce with the streams of Styx. The darkness is full of fantastic spectres, with horrid looks and piteous cries: judges, torturers, abysses, gulfs crammed with innumerable woes. (167A)

[15] Euripides, *Orestes* 211.

Atheism, the lack of belief in the gods, is by contrast a less serious thing, an intellectual error not aggravated by this emotional trauma.

Yet nobody who reads Plutarch or thinks of his career can doubt for a moment that he was a pious believer, or that he thought it at any rate a reasonable hope to trust in another life and happiness therein for the virtuous. Explicit statements are not hard to find; here is one from one of the polemics against the Epicureans:

In destroying the belief in immortality, the Epicureans destroy the sweetest and greatest hopes of the mass of mankind. What are we to believe of the good, who have lived pious and upright lives and expect no evil yonder but only things most lovely and divine? Athletes receive their prizes not during the contest but after they have won. Similarly, the belief that the prizes of victory in life are reserved for the good when life is over makes people feel a marvellous enthusiasm for virtue in the light of these expectations, which embrace also the spectacle of the due punishment of such persons as now take advantage of power and wealth to be arrogant and thoughtlessly contemptuous of their superiors. Secondly: no lover of these things succeeds in satisfying himself on earth with truth and the vision of reality. Our reason is befogged and confused in the mist or cloud, as it were, of the body. Man looks upwards, in hope of flying bird-like from the body to something grand and splendid; and philosophy is his practice for death. (1105C ff.)

Superstition certainly seems to strike a different note from these other-worldly echoes of the *Phaedo*. Two explanations of the contrast have commonly been put forward. One is that *Superstition* is one of a pair of pieces the other of which would deal similarly with atheism. This has little plausibility; what we have is clearly a comparison between the two vices, with the neat Aristotelian conclusion that they are the extremes corresponding to the 'mean', which is piety. The other and commoner view is that Plutarch changed his mind and became more pious as he grew older, and that *Superstition* is an unusually early work. There is no independent argument for this, and it is circular to deduce difference of date from difference of doctrine. The most probable solution is that we must try to reconcile the two points of view. Nor is this so difficult after all. The prospect of rewards after death is only a hope; but what is certain, and removes all cause for panic, is the fairness and goodness of God. The atheist is a fool, the superstitious man is impious:

I would rather have people say there is no such person as Plutarch than that Plutarch is an unstable, changeable character, quick to anger, vindictive over trivialities, and easily offended. (170A)

The Platonist theme of the essential reliability and goodness of God is the key to Plutarch's attitude to religion. 'Rest content,' he seems to say, 'with the hopes that philosophy and religion extend; we all know we can't be dogmatic about it.'

It follows that the right interpretation of cult and myth was of central importance. For a man of civilised morals and conservative inclinations confronting the bizarre heritage of Greek and barbarian practice and legend, this raises at once the possibility of allegory. Now allegory had a long history in Greek speculation,[16] and both Platonists and Stoics had attended to it, and for more or less the same motives, since both parties habitually liked to conserve tradition, to exploit the wisdom of the poets, and to show respect to science and learning. Stoic treatments of the subject were particularly ingenious; the extant first-century treatises of Cornutus and 'Heraclitus' are good examples, and Plutarch certainly knows and uses work like theirs. The general principle of allegorical interpretation was not a sectarian matter. What mattered was good sense in employing it and regard to the canons of decency and morality. Where Plutarch criticises the interpretation of others, it is on these grounds that he does it. 'Myths must be handled not as if they were factual statements'— *logoi*: the *logos-muthos* contrast is Plato's—'but by adopting out of each what is *appropriate*, on the principle of likeness' (374E). Euhemerist readings of myth inevitably contravene this (360A); Euhemerus 'spread atheism through the world' by degrading the

---

[16] A good brief account by J. Tate, *Oxford Classical Dictionary*, s.v. Allegory.

gods of common belief into supposed historical characters. This was the ultimate neglect of propriety, an over-riding of the most important status-rule of all. Purely physical allegory is often, though not necessarily, wrong for similar reasons. For instance, it is wrong to explain the improper story of Ares' adultery with Aphrodite, an old stumbling-block in the use of Homer as a moral educator, in astrological terms as 'Mars in conjunction with Venus portending adulterous births' (19E). More explicitly, in *Isis and Osiris*:

It is not right to think of Osiris or Isis as water or sun or earth or sky, nor of Typhon as fire or drought or sea. If we are to avoid error, we must attribute to Typhon anything in these which lacks due measure or order on account of some excess or defect, while we honour and respect the ordered, good and useful as the handiwork of Isis and the image, reproduction and principle of Osiris. (376F)

It ought to follow that Plutarch should not seriously put forward a physical explanation as the last word on a problem of the evaluation of myth or cult. In *The Daedala at Plataea*,[17] an account of a local Boeotian ritual involving an aniconic wooden cult-object, the surviving fragment speaks with approval of a 'physical' explanation as 'appropriate'. It also includes an allegory in which Zeus represents a 'hot fiery force'. This last point is clearly Stoic. Since the passage seems to be a speech addressed to an audience of several people, the conclusion that it is a speech in a dialogue is justified. It need not therefore represent Plutarch's own opinion, and it does not disturb the general picture.

Allegory was thus a main method of justifying to a literate and in some ways very sophisticated public the teachings and cult-practices of a traditional religion which went back to very much more primitive ways of thinking. It also fulfilled the function of interpreting non-Greek religions and integrating them into the general framework of an acceptable philosophical attitude to the gods. For Plutarch's *theologia* did not confine itself to the Hellenic range. Roman cult was naturally a major interest; his wide reading

17 Fr. 157 Sandbach.

in the antiquities of this subject is displayed both in the *Lives* and in the very learned collection of *problēmata* called *Roman Questions*. Of the newer cults that were spreading through the cities and armies of the Mediterranean world, he says nothing of Christianity, still an affair of a few scattered communities; and nothing, more surprisingly, of Mithraism, though he had some knowledge of Zoroastrian ideas. He does however discuss the Jews;[18] there was a fair amount of gentile literature on Jewish matters. He talks not only of their food taboos but of the identity of their god. The Athenian Moiragenes (671C) is made to adduce various proofs from cult that the Jews in fact worship Dionysus; and if it were permitted to reveal the mystical teaching of Eleusis, he would, he claims, be able to adduce more. But Plutarch's most important excursion into non-Greek religion is the great treatise *Isis and Osiris*. In this, his characteristic dualistic Platonism is applied to the interpretation of Egyptian myth. The Isiac and the Platonist join in a fascinating synthesis; was Apuleius perhaps thinking of this when he made the initiate-hero of the *Metamorphoses* a kinsman of Plutarch?

In all this, as in the interpretation of philosophical texts, moral concern and learning go hand in hand. The learning often seems formal and pedantic, and expresses itself in the stereotyped sentences of the commentator, but it also involves vast reading and sometimes a shrewd philosophical or anthropological judgment. In the accumulation of *historia*, Plutarch resembles his character Cleombrotus; where he differs from him is in bringing the resulting *theologia* under the critical control of morality, propriety, and reason. In this, his thought shows some analogy with his literary position. We saw that in language and style he represents the old order, the continuous tradition, not the new archaism of the international sophistic that followed. Similarly in matters of religion: he belongs to the continuous tradition of Hellenic piety and Hellenic scepticism, not much affected by the great changes in religious feeling which he could sense in the world around.

[18] e.g. *Table Talk* 4.4–6; *Isis and Osiris* 363C.

CHAPTER FIVE

The Moralist and his Fellow-men

PLUTARCH was a Platonist also in his ethics. He polemises against Stoic extravagances: the paradox of the parity of errors, the ideal of immunity to emotion (*apatheia*). The most comprehensive of his surviving ethical works, *Moral Virtue* (440D) is essentially such a polemic. Platonist in substance, Aristotelian in much of its terminology, it testifies to the fact that the detail of moral theory and the norm for its presentation were inherited not from the Academy but from the Lyceum. The beginning of the book states Plato's psychology clearly. The Stoics failed to see that there is a division within the soul where the 'rational' and 'ir-rational' or 'non-rational' (*alogon*) elements are related in some-what the same way as 'soul' itself to 'body'. Pythagoras had understood this, for it was implied in his use of music in education to charm the 'non-rational'. It was Plato however who made the theory explicit. For him, the 'world soul' was a complex of 'the same' and 'the other', and the human soul (says Plutarch) a part or copy of this, constructed on a similar formula, and containing both an element of 'intelligence and calculation' and one of 'emotion and irrationality'. The latter is itself divided into the elements familiar from the *Republic*, the 'desiderative' (*epithu-mētikon*) and the spirited (*thumoeides*). This account, which is naturally not original with Plutarch but goes back to the early Academy, is indeed unfair to the special insight of the *Republic*. Even if he did not follow it up very much, Plato had there seen the human drive to action as something qualitatively different both from desire and from rational calculation. The commonsense simplification closes the road to a more developed psychology. 'Moral goodness' for Plutarch is a quality of the whole 'irrational' soul defined and fashioned by 'reason'. Its 'matter' is emotion, reason is its 'form'. It is properly described, as Aristotle described it, as a 'mean' (*mesotēs*) between 'excesses' and 'defects'. So 'piety' is a 'mean', between superstition and atheism, and 'prudence' (66c) a 'mean' between unscrupulousness and stupidity. The most important questions for Plutarch are naturally the practical ones. How far and by what means can this emotional order be imposed? How can the *mesotēs* be secured? Not only many of the treatises in the *Moralia* but in a sense the *Lives* as a whole are concerned with this. The biographer provides documented and instructive case-studies of the play of reason and emotion. The more we know of the detail of a life, the more clearly we can see the process and effect of the moulding of the one by the other.

But, first, what are the limits of improvement? Plutarch believed there were good men, and perhaps even hoped to be one; but he did not believe in the perfectibility of human nature or in the total control of the irrational by *logos*. There are limits to what can be done, and they are set by the nature of the *kosmos* and of God's power in it.

In *God's Slowness to Punish*, Plutarch seems to set out the position in a speech which he puts in his own mouth. In one passage (551c ff.) he is seeking to justify God's apparent reluctance to inflict punishment:

It is likely (*eikos*) that if God lays hand in justice on a sick soul, he discerns its emotional condition, and sees if this yields in any way and gives scope for repentance. He can fix the timing too, so long as the vice is not unrelieved and intractable. For he knows what share (*moira*) of virtue souls acquire from him when they proceed to birth, and how strong and indelible is their natural nobility, though it breaks out in a rash of vice against its nature if corrupted by bad education or bad company, and may subsequently recover its appropriate condition as a result of good treatment. For this reason he does not hasten everyone's punishment at the same rate. What is incurable, he removes from life and cuts off, because the constant association with moral evil is inevitably harmful to others and most harmful of all to the person himself. On the other hand, where it seems probable that the tendency to error arises from ignorance of good rather than from choice of evil, he grants time for change; if the sinner persists, he executes the sentence; he has, to be sure, no reason to be apprehensive of an escape.

Consider how many changes occur in the character (*ēthos*) and life of men. This is why the variable element is called *tropos* ('turn', 'way') and *ēthos*, because *ĕthos* (habit) enters deeply into it, grips it and controls it. The ancients, in my view of it, called Cecrops 'double-natured' not, as some say, because he turned from a good king into a fierce and dragon-like tyrant, but because, though crooked and terrible to begin with, he subsequently ruled with gentleness and humanity . . .

Various other historical examples follow; we recall also the Theseus and the Pericles of the *Lives* both of whom changed as a result of the experience of rule.[1] A few pages later comes the following (562B–D):

It is a task for divine wisdom, not for human, to discern and perceive innate similarities and differences before they make themselves obvious by falling into serious crime through some access of emotion. The young of bears, wolves and monkeys display their character from the very beginning in infancy, with nothing to disguise or modify it; human nature, on the other hand, by entering as it does into habits, opinions and conventions, frequently conceals its evil and mimics the good, with the result that it either succeeds in wiping out and so escaping altogether its innate stain of vice, or else at least escapes detection for a long time under a sort of blanket of unscrupulousness; it may even escape the notice of those of us who ultimately and reluctantly reach an understanding of the underlying vice from the individual blows and stings of particular vicious acts—or, to be more accurate, believe that people become unjust only when they commit injustice, licentious only when they actually perform some outrageous act, cowardly only when they actually run away. One might as well believe that scorpions grow their stings when they strike, and vipers their venom when they bite. This is a silly notion, for people do not in fact acquire their wickedness

---

[1] *Comparison of Theseus and Romulus* 2.

and display it at the same moment. The thief and the potential tyrant have their foible from the beginning, but activate it only when they find opportunity and power. But God of course knows the disposition and nature of us all, because his nature is to perceive the mind rather than the body. He does not wait till violence is in the hands, impudence in the voice, and licentiousness in the sexual organs, before inflicting punishment. He is not retaliating upon the wrongdoer as one wronged, nor growing angry with the robber as a victim, nor hating the adulterer as an injured party. Instead, he often chastises the mere tendency to adultery, rapacity or wrongdoing, removing the vice before it attacks, as one would take precautions against a seizure.

These passages between them seem to contain the essentials of Plutarch's convictions about the nature of man and his capacity for improvement. It is a sombre but not despairing creed. We are apparently liable to be punished for tendencies to vice which we have inherited but concealed all our lives. Yet there is a possibility of escape: habit, right opinions, the observance of the conventions of a healthy society, may wipe away the taint altogether. And we inherit—or bring from God, as Plutarch puts it, in terms which sound mythical but may well represent precise belief—not only evil but goodness; only it is a goodness which, by a reverse process, may be corrupted by habits or bad company, with the result that we sin 'contrary to our nature'.

It follows that the all-important thing is the proper use of education and environment, not of course to conceal evil but to strengthen the good tendencies and eradicate the pernicious. How the heroes of history succeeded or failed in this is a main subject of the *Lives*. In a more general way, *Progress in Virtue* (75A) handles the same theme. The good life is a conversion, the completeness of which is known only to the individual—and presumably to God:

The lover of beauty and wisdom, who in his actions consorts with virtue and follows her ways, may be expected to keep his lofty thoughts quietly to himself, and to need no panegyrist or audience. (80E)

The conversion is a gradual one, and this is a point that again sets

Plutarch in at least formal opposition to the Stoics, for whom everything except perfect wisdom is strictly speaking folly and vice, and conversion therefore instantaneous. In practice of course the Stoics are not so different; the picture and the theory of moral improvement that we get from Seneca's correspondence with Lucilius is not so very remote from Plutarch's. *Progress in Virtue* gives indeed a clear enough view. Later than the formal polemics against the Stoa, it is addressed to Sosius Senecio, the recipient also of the *Parallel Lives*. The question it poses is how we can recognise our own or another's progress—*prokopē*, a Stoic term. There are a number of diagnostic signs (82B): willingness to accept correction; abatement of emotion; the growth of a positive desire to obey the dictates of reason; a genuine admiration for good men, with no contamination of jealousy; the habitual use of the example of good men; finally, the scrupulousness in little things that is indicative of care in greater.

And how can we actually make this progress? Morality, like any other skill, depends on theory and on practice.[2] Theory is represented by knowing and having ready to mind 'useful thoughts' (*chrēsimoi epilogismoi*, 532D). Practice consists of exercises conducive to the formation of good habits. Plutarch's moral advice covers both these heads. In both, he is following a long tradition, common to all the Hellenistic schools, with only minor differences of emphasis and practice. Exercise (*askēsis*) fulfils the same function in the acquisition of mental health as gymnastics do for the body. The patient begins with comparatively easy exercises and progresses to the more difficult. If you suffer from curiosity (*polupragmosunē*), train yourself by not reading inscriptions on tombs or scribblings on walls, by not peering into other people's houses, by not sidling up to people who are quarrelling to find out what is going on (515B). If your trouble is an inhibiting shyness or unwillingness to say no—the

---

[2] A recent work which discusses the methods of 'cure' propounded in a number of Plutarch's treatises is H. G. Ingenkamp, *Plutarchs Schriften über die Heilung der Seele*, 1971.

failing Plutarch calls *dusōpia* (528c)—you should begin by some little act of will, like refusing another round of drinks or getting rid of a bore. This will help you in more important problems another time—for example it will make it easier to refuse a friend something in which it would be harmful to oblige him. Resisting the importunate is a virtue in the influential. Anger was the most studied of the vices; Plutarch's treatise on its control (452E) gives the fullest treatment of this technique of precept and habituation. But some of the extensions of the principle come to very unconvincing results: does it really constitute practice for 'justice' to refuse a sum of money to which you have every right (524A)?

The process—as this last example makes especially clear—is self-centred in much the same way as physical exercise. Where other people come into it, they are not considered for their own sake, but as means to the individual's perfection. So (459B) do not be angry with slaves or treat animals harshly. You have the power of course, and no obvious disaster will follow if you indulge it. But you will have lowered yourself and lost the capacity to restrain anger and cruelty in other and more important contexts. Worst of all, you will have missed a chance of weakening the 'taint' in your soul.

But to emphasise this is to risk getting the picture wrong. It is not the self-centredness of his moral ideal that is peculiar to Plutarch. On the contrary, that is a common inheritance. No pagan moralist sees the love or service of others as in itself at the top of the scale of goods. Perhaps the Stoics, with their ideal of submission to an order both rational and natural, embracing the community of gods and men, came nearest to the notion of self-sacrifice as an end; but it was a very special kind of self-sacrifice, since it was also the fulfilment of the highest element in human nature. To the Platonist or Aristotelian, *eudaimonia* ('felicity') is self-evidently the goal. It may involve preferring honour to pleasure, death to disgrace, restraint to indulgence. But it can never lead one to think of the *eudaimonia* of some other person as to be preferred to one's own. What is notable in Plutarch is not his adhesion to these attitudes, but his tacit modifications of them. These come from the emphasis laid in all his moral judgments on mildness and humanity, *prāotēs* and *philanthrōpia*; these are qualities which, even if practised in a self-regarding sense, involve at least some degree of concern and understanding for the feelings and aims of others. What we may call Plutarch's social ethics displays this in many ways; notably in his writings on sex, love and family.

We saw[3] that the famous *Consolation* on his daughter's death has a predominantly hortatory tone, a warning against feminine superstition. Yet much humanity shines out of its moralism, and there are few passages in ancient literature to touch the sentiment of this remembrance of a dead child (608C–D):

Our affection for children of that age gains extra piquancy from the real purity of the pleasure they give, the absence of any crossness or complaint. She had by nature a quite extraordinary contentment and mildness of temper, and the way she reciprocated love and offered favours gave one not only pleasure but an understanding of the human feeling (*philanthrōpia*) in her heart. She used to ask her nurse to offer the breast not only to other children but to the playthings and toys she loved, and invited them as it were to her own table, sharing her goods out of kindness of heart and giving part of her pleasures to whatever gave her joy.

The same sort of mixture of moral austerity and natural sentiment marks the comparatively early work *Advice on Marriage* (138A). This is in form unique among Plutarch's extant writings: it consists of a collection of similes or comparisons, each with a lesson, with only a modest amount of connected argument. Preface and peroration however make the general drift clear. This is advice for a philosophic marriage, in which the husband is also the teacher. The idea of such a union goes back at least to the Socratics,[4] and a Cynic version of it is to be seen in the 'correspondence' of Crates and Hipparchia.[5] Education by the

---

[3] Above, p. 78.   [4] Xenophon, *Symposium* 2.9.
[5] *Epistolographi Graeci*, ed. R. Hercher, 208 ff.; Crates was a disciple of Diogenes, but the letters are a fiction, presumably of the imperial age.

husband, Plutarch thinks, will protect the woman against extravagant behaviour. 'If she knows geometry, she will be ashamed to dance' (145C)—in orgiastic rites, to judge from the context, rather than as a social accomplishment. She is bidden to keep the sayings of famous men in her mind and have on her lips the wisdom Plutarch taught her, to follow the patterns set by virtuous and wise women of old, and to share not in Sappho's 'roses of Pieria' but in the fruit the Muses bear and bestow on those who respect education and philosophy. In other words, she is to make 'moral progress' by the commonly recommended method of 'useful thoughts'. With this dominant theme, however, is linked a subordinate but more congenial one: emphasis on kindliness of character (*ēthos*), on avoiding quarrels, on loyalty and faithfulness, love and affection.

In some ways Plutarch's attitude recalls that of his older contemporary, the Stoic Musonius Rufus.[6] According to Musonius, women deserve education and are capable of it, while marriage is natural, necessary for the species, an essential foundation of family, state, and world-community, and the source of a very special kind of friendship (*philia*). Plutarch is unlikely to have been influenced by Musonius, though he quotes remarks of his once or twice in other contexts.[7] In fact, he differs from him very considerably. He does not have the social argument that marriage is a basis of society. And he does attach—in quite a different vein from Musonius—a high moral value to sexual pleasure within marriage. This is a significant difference. It seems to show Plutarch more closely in touch with common feeling than the Stoic, closer in fact to the common sentiments that we find in the unphilosophical morality of Greece from the time of Menander onwards. The standards of loyalty and faithfulness are valid for both sexes, the husband's duties as strict as the wife's. *Advice on Marriage* at least lets us glimpse this side of things. Pollianus and Eurydice, the couple to whom it is addressed, may be philosophers, but they are allowed to be human as well.

[6] See A. C. van Geytenbeek, *Musonius Rufus*, 1963, 51–77.
[7] 453D, 830B.

Marriage is also a main theme of the later and much more elaborate *Book of Love* (748E). The debates in this dialogue are linked in subject to its novelistic setting, the story of the young man of Thespiae carried off into matrimony by the rich widow. They cover three topics. First comes a *sunkrisis* of homosexual and heterosexual love, to the advantage of the latter. Here is Plutarch pleading an anti-Platonic, almost anti-philosophical cause; once again he is on the side of the ordinary, humane morality of Greece. The second question, whether love is a god, echoes Plato's *Symposium*; it gains in interest by being asked at the festival of Eros at Thespiae, one of the few famous cults of the god anywhere in Greece. Third come the arguments in favour of marriage:

With the married, sex is the beginning of affection (*philia*, 'friendship'). It is like a joint participation in some great ceremony. The pleasure itself is not important. It is the respect and grace and contentment with each other and the confidence that springs from this that shows the Delphians were right to call Aphrodite 'Arma' ('union' or 'harmony') and Homer to use the word *philotēs* ('friendliness') for this kind of association. It shows too that Solon was a very experienced legislator in matters connubial, when he ordained that one should make love to one's wife at least three times a month—not of course for the pleasure of it, but because he wanted the marriage to be renewed by such lovingness after the differences which inevitably accumulate, rather as cities renew peace-treaties between themselves periodically . . . This union of loving partners is the real 'total mixture'. Any other kind of joint life is like the Epicurean 'contacts' and 'embraces', an affair of collisions and rebounds, that fails to produce the sort of unity that love effects when he puts his hand to a union in marriage. No greater pleasures come from others, no more continuous services are due to others; no other friendship possesses so notable and enviable an element of esteem as when

a man and a woman
dwell in their house together, united in mind. (769A, F)

This quotation from the *Odyssey* (6.183) is naturally a stock part of any reflections on marriage. The rest of the ornamentation is more recondite and characteristic of Plutarch's allusiveness and ingenuity. 'Total mixture' is a Stoic technical term (*di' holōn krāsis*). Both this and the Epicurean technicalities that follow are in a sense pure ornament, but as often there is a special significance in the imagery. Here it derives from the fact that the Epicureans were both atomists and hedonists; there is a point therefore in using the terms of their physical theories to illustrate the superficial, self-indulgent type of association. Most important is the colour given to the whole passage by subsuming the marriage-bond under the general head of *philia*. The traditional distinction between the three kinds of *philia*—those of pleasure, service, and esteem or virtue—obviously underlies the argument, and especially the clinching sentence that leads up to the lines of Homer.

This way of looking at the subject is of course perfectly natural. In their social aspect, love and marriage are indeed special sorts of *philia*. This is a wider concept than the English 'friendship'. On the one hand it denotes any kind of affinity or close association; on the other, like the Latin *amicitia*, it implies an overt relationship of duties and expectations which may, but need not, involve a warm feeling of affection.

Philia was in fact a large topic in Greek ethics, and a specially important one to Plutarch. The classic texts were Plato's *Lysis* and still more Aristotle's *Ethics*. As usual it was Aristotle who systematised and created the terminology of later discussions. He was the formulator of the three-fold classification of *philia* that Plutarch plays with in the passage we have been considering; the primary friendship, on Aristotle's view, was produced by virtue, the others by considerations of utility and pleasure. A whole casuistry of *philia* was developed. Does the good man need friends? Should one try to acquire many friends? Can one be one's own friend? These and similar *topoi* admitted stock arguments on both sides.

Many of these *topoi* are to be found in Plutarch too. *Poluphilia*, the acquisition of many friends, which the Stoics treated as a good, is the subject of one essay, in which the Stoic position is, of course, rebutted. The possession of many friends is seen to be a symptom of an inconstant character. True friendship is mating, not herding. Its currency is good will and gratitude in a context of virtue. This is once again Aristotle's first type of *philia*, to which reciprocal good will (*eunoia*) is essential. Plutarch concludes (96E) with a characteristic passage of allusion and imagery:

Who then is so industrious, so variable, so manifold to make himself resemble many different people, to adapt himself to them, to take seriously the advice in Theognis:

> Model your mind on the sensible polypus
> who makes himself look like the rock that he clings to?

Yet the polypus' variations have no third dimension. They affect only the creature's surface, which admits the effluences of adjacent objects according to density or looseness of texture. Friendships on the other hand seek to produce an assimilation of character, emotions, ideas, habits and dispositions. This leads to the procedure of a Proteus, unhappy and wicked, changing himself repeatedly by magic from one thing to another. With scholars he reads, with wrestlers he tries a fall, with the hunting folk he runs with the hounds, with the drunkards he gets drunk, with the politicians he campaigns for office. He has no focal character of his own. Scientists tell us that the unfigured substance or matter, that underlies qualities and is changed by them, burns at one moment, is liquefied at another, or aerified, or solidified; similarly, underneath the 'friend of many' must lie a mind of many passions and changes, pliant and variable. But real friendship seeks a stable, firm, unchanging character of single place and habit. This is why a firm friend is a rare object and hard to find.

In other words, the 'friend of many' acquires the instability of character that goes with insincere friendship. He can in fact hardly be distinguished from a more familiar figure of the moralists, the *kolax* or flatterer, the fake friend—so hard—and so important—to distinguish from the true.

Friends and Flatterers (48E) is in fact Plutarch's most considerable work in this field. It is obviously based on a long tradition. Theophrastus is generally supposed to be its chief source. Other Peripatetics like Clearchus are also probably involved, and there are close similarities with Cicero's Stoic authority Panaetius. The structure is crude, and the work looks like two separate pieces stuck together: the debating issue 'How can we tell a flatterer from a friend?' and a self-contained essay on frank speaking (*parrhēsia*). Both parts make a good deal of use of the tripartite division of *philia*. The influence of Plato also is pervasive: the book begins with a Platonic quotation, and the theme of demagogues as *kolakes* goes back to the *Gorgias*. Most of the imagery and material is, as usual, classical; but the *exempla* extend down to Antony and Nero.

How is the *kolax* recognised?

Having no single and abiding focal character, not living the life of his choice for himself but for another, moulding and modelling himself on another, he is not a single individual but manifold and various, always running into new shapes like water transferred from one vessel to another, taking shape from the container. Owls are caught walking and dancing, evidently attempting to imitate men; flatterers actually seduce and ensnare others by their imitations. They do not indeed follow the same procedure with everyone. With some they dance and sing, with others they wrestle and sprinkle dust on themselves. If a flatterer lays hold on a hunting enthusiast, you can almost hear him chanting Phaedra's song as he goes along:

> I'm in love with hallooing to the hounds,
> as we chase the dappled deer.[8]

If it's a scholar or a young student that he's after, he is deep in his books, grows a beard to his feet; it's all gowns and indifference to circumstance; his talk runs on numbers and right-angled triangles. But suppose a rich, lazy drunkard comes his way:

> Then wily Odysseus strips off his rags.

Off goes the gown, off comes the beard like a poor harvest. And what do we find instead? Wine-cups and bowls, laughter in the public walks, and jokes at the expense of the philosophers . . . Further evidence comes from the activity of those great *kolakes* the demagogues. The

---

[8] Euripides, *Hippolytus* 218.

chief of these was Alcibiades. At Athens, he was humorous, kept horses, and lived with elegance and grace. At Sparta, he shaved close, wore a cloak, and took cold baths. In Thrace, he was a warrior and a drinker. When he went to see Tissaphernes, he displayed luxury, delicacy and pretentiousness. And so he won the allegiance and friendship of them all by making himself like them. Not so Epaminondas and Agesilaus: though they too had dealings with many men and many countries and many ways of life, they everywhere preserved their own personalities in dress, habits, speech, and style of living. (52A–F)

The treatment of the subject in this passage illustrates not only the free transfer of descriptive detail between *kolax* and *poluphilos*, but also the intimate links between private morals and historical and political judgments. The ideal heroes Epaminondas and Agesilaus are here moral *exempla*, opposed to the turncoat Alcibiades. Plutarch wrote the biographies of all three. The *topos* of Alcibiades' chameleon-like changes of life-style is developed in the *Life* almost in these terms; Plutarch did not invent all this, it is part of the Alcibiades legend.[9]

Philia is a topic of social morals, and it has clear connections, especially in the Roman world, with public life. Plutarch's late essay *How to Profit from Your Enemies* (86B) belongs thematically to the group of works on friendship, but it is closer than the others to the world of politics. The addressee, Cornelius Pulcher, has ambitions in imperial affairs. He has chosen, we are told, the mildest (*prāotaton*) style of public life. But he must be warned that he cannot expect to avoid jealousy, envy and contentiousness, which all breed hatred. He will inevitably have enemies; let him learn to profit from them. This is an old theme, in fact it is out of Xenophon.[10] Various moral commonplaces prove relevant to it: the value of difficulties, the use of clear-sighted and even hostile criticism, the stimulus of rivalry. Enemies provide a golden opportunity for the exercise of self-control. Restrain your temper in dealing with them as practice for dealing with your friends, where it matters much more. Here again is the familiar advocacy of self-regarding *askēsis* (91E):

[9] See below, pp. 108, 123.　　　[10] *Oeconomicus* 1.15.

As Simonides says, 'every lark must have a crest'. So every human personality carries contentiousness, envy and malice, that 'comrade of the vain in mind' as Pindar puts it. Consequently, one can obtain very considerable benefit by discharging these emotions on one's enemies and turning the stream as it were as far as possible from friends and connections.

How to Profit from Your Enemies assumes a knowledge of *Advice on Public Life* (798A), the closest in content of any of the *Moralia* both to specific contemporary issues and to the historical researches which Plutarch undertook primarily for the *Lives*. *Advice* is addressed to a young citizen of Sardis, Menemachus, who intends to go into politics. The limitations of power in a Roman province are realistically, even brutally, described. There is practical advice on tactics and style of speech; though no textbook of rhetoric, the book owes much to rhetorical teaching. But there is also a strong moral tone. Once again, the true statesman is contrasted with the inconsistent and self-interested *kolax*, and the statesman must set an example of virtuous and level-headed life. Within the limits set by the ruling power, there is scope for policies that can display the qualities of virtue and humanity, and continue the Hellenic tradition (814A):

There are many passages in the earlier history of Greece which may be used to control the attitudes and feelings of the present. At Athens, we can remind the *dēmos* not of its military past, but, for example, of the decree of amnesty for the Thirty, or the fine imposed on Phrynichus for his play about the capture of Miletus . . . or how, when houses were being searched at the time of the Harpalus affair, they exempted the house of the newly married couple . . .

The closing passage is a plea for the peaceful virtues (824D):

What remains for the statesman is the single task—though it is as important as any—of ensuring peace and concord among his fellow-citizens, and removing all strife, dissension and hostility. He should proceed as one would do in reconciling friends: first conciliating the aggrieved and giving the impression of sharing their grievance, then trying to calm them down and convince them that those who pass over wrongs are superior to those who strive to win by force not only in decency and good nature (*epieikeia, ēthos*) but in spirit and greatness of mind. Yielding in small things, they prevail (he should say) in the greatest and most honourable.

What is here advocated for the subject Greeks, and with emphasis on their weakness, is also something that in Plutarch's view is to be commended among all conditions of men and in all ages. Kindness and all the gentler and more humane forms of *aretē*, are of the essence of the good life. Without them, courage becomes mere aggressiveness and ends in brutality. This is a recurrent theme of the *Lives*; *Marius* is an outstanding example. Humanity, to Plutarch's way of thinking, was something that Greek education could contribute to a world governed by the potentially destructive force of Roman armies.[11] Man's highest praise comes not from conquest and power, but from beneficence. The encomium at the end of the life of Pericles seems to come from the heart:

'No Athenian,' he said, 'ever put on mourning by my doing.' Pericles deserves our admiration, not only for the fairness and mildness (*epieikeia, prāotēs*) that he consistently maintained amid many difficulties and great hatreds, but also for the pride that made him regard as the chief of his achievements the fact that, with all that power, he had never given way to jealousy or anger, or regarded any of his enemies as incurably hostile. The nickname 'Olympian'[12] was childish and vain; but there is one consideration that makes it unexceptionable and appropriate, and that is that it was applied to a character so benevolent and a life so pure and unsullied in a position of power. We believe that the gods, who are rulers and monarchs of the world, are responsible for good things but not for evil. The poets indeed try to confuse us with their ignorant opinions, but their own fables refute them. The place where they say the gods dwell they describe as a safe, unshaken seat, vexed by no wind or cloud, perpetually shining with a gentle serenity of sky and a pure

[11] See, e.g., *Galba* 1, *Comparison of Pelopidas and Marcellus* 1, *Comparison of Numa and Lycurgus* 4.
[12] Aristophanes, *Acharnians* 530.

light; such, they suppose, are the surroundings that best suit the blessed and immortal. Yet they describe the gods themselves as full of confusion, malice, anger, and other emotions inappropriate even in sensible humans! (39)

CHAPTER SIX

An Introduction to the 'Lives'[1]

IN writing biography, Plutarch lighted on a literary genre which both suited his talents and disguised some of his limitations. His immense breadth of reading, his moralist's and teacher's view of society and history, and his talent for vivid and evocative narrative found the scope they needed. At the same time, the tendency to irrelevance and looseness of structure which is evident in many places in the *Moralia* was held in check by a form in which shape and scale were firmly prescribed by the material and the professed purpose. Plutarch came to think of the *Parallel Lives* as the major enterprise of his career. Conscious of this, he often expounds his motives and methods. The work was begun, he tells us in the preface to *Timoleon*, 'for the sake of others', in other words for their improvement—though not necessarily at their instigation[2] —and continued 'for his own sake', because it seemed to offer moral lessons that the writer too might apply in his own life. In the preface to *Pericles* (1–2) he spells out the educational theory even more clearly:

Since the mind naturally possesses a love of learning and contemplation, it is surely reasonable to blame people who misuse this on entertainments for eye or ear that are of no serious value, while they neglect the noble and the useful . . . As the eye is suited by a colour whose

---

[1] There are a number of studies with a similar scope to this chapter: A. W. Gomme, *Thucydides I*, 54–84; J. R. Hamilton, *Plutarch's 'Alexander'*, xxxiii ff.; A. J. Gossage in *Latin Biography*, ed. T. A. Dorey, 45–78; D. A. Russell, *Greece and Rome* 13 (1966) 139 ff.; C. P. Jones, *Plutarch and Rome*, 72–109; A. E. Wardman, *CQ* 21 (1971) 254 ff.

[2] It is (I now think) an error to regard the *Lives* as the 'command' of Senecio or anyone else.

brightness and pleasantness revives and nurtures the sight, so must we bring our minds to spectacles that tempt them to their own proper good by way of enjoyment. We find this in the actions of virtue. These give the inquirer an admiration and an enthusiasm that leads him to imitate. In other spheres, the impulse to action does not immediately follow admiration of the act . . . No young man of talent wants to become a Phidias because he has seen the Zeus at Pisa, or a Polyclitus because of the Hera at Argos, or an Anacreon or Philemon or Archilochus because he enjoys their poems. For it does not follow that because the work is pretty and gives delight the workman is necessarily worth serious regard. Hence there is no benefit to the spectator in such things, because no imitative zeal arises in connection with them, nor any upsurge of feeling giving rise to enthusiastic impulses towards assimilation with the object. Virtue, however, instantly produces by her actions a frame of mind in which the deed is admired and the doer rivalled at one and the same moment . . . Nobility (*to kalon*; perhaps 'moral beauty') exercises an active attraction and immediately creates an active impulse, not merely forming the eye-witness's personality by imitation, but producing a settled moral choice (*prohairesis*) from the simple historical knowledge of the action. This is why I have made up my mind to spend my time writing biographies, and have composed this Tenth Book, comprising the lives of Pericles and of the Fabius Maximus who fought the war against Hannibal.

In the preface to *Timoleon*, Plutarch used the rather emotive verb *philochōrein* ('to be home-keeping') for his perseverance in biography; it is the word he uses also for his choosing to live out his days in his native Chaeronea.[3] Biography proved his literary home. Not that he gave up other writing. The chronology[4] remains uncertain. It is only a conjecture that Sosius Senecio's consulship in 99 was the occasion of the dedication of the enterprise to him. Many of the miscellaneous works clearly date from the period when the *Lives* were being written. There are many links both ways.

Bion graphein, 'to write a life', carries connotations alien to modern concepts of biography. The differences are important

---

[3] *Demosthenes* 2 (above, p. 1).
[4] The standard work is C. Stoltz, *Zur relativen Chronologie der Parallelbiographien Plutarchs*, 1929.

if we are to understand what Plutarch intended. *Bios* means, roughly, 'way of life', whether in an individual or in a society; Dicaearchus, a pupil of Aristotle, wrote a kind of general social history under the title *Bios Hellados*. It also has some connotations of *ordinary* life, and is associated with the realism of comedy[5] rather than with the grand topics of epic or, for that matter, history. *Bios* is the word Aristophanes of Byzantium used in the lines:

> O *Life*! O Menander!
> Which of you took the copy of the other?[6]

Thus to describe the *bios* of a great man was to say 'what sort of man he was' (*poios tis ēn*) and to regard him, in a sense, as one of ourselves. One might almost say also that biography stood to history as the comedy of manners stood to tragedy.

From this follow three characteristics of ancient biography which are central to the understanding of Plutarch.

One is that chronology and development in time are of secondary concern even though the overall arrangement—unlike for example that of Suetonius—is chronologically straightforward. There is here a marked contrast with modern ways. For the biographer today, time is perhaps the most important dimension of his subject. Not only does the man mature and decay; the world he moves in is also continually changing, and this has to be made clear whenever one can. In Plutarch, both the hero and the general historical conditions have a fixed nature and remain comparatively static. It is easy to miss this, because the events are often exciting and dramatic and the elements of which the *bios* is made up are very much those with which the modern biographer also operates. Childhood anecdotes, education, emergence into public life, conflicts, responses to the challenge of circumstances, are always the stuff of the book; but the question which is being answered all along is the rather unsophisticated 'What sort of man was he?' that could almost find adequate answer in a series

---

[5] cf. 'Longinus' 9.15 on the *Odyssey*.
[6] Syrianus, *Comm. in Hermogenem* 2.23 Rabe.

of descriptive adjectives. The facts are therefore presented not so much for their intrinsic interest as in evidence to support a general judgement. The preface to *Pericles* continues:

These men resembled each other generally in their virtues, but especially in their mildness (*prāotēs*) and uprightness. Both did the greatest service to their countries by their capacity to endure the foolishness of their peoples (*dēmoi*) and of their colleagues in office. Whether this is a right judgment or not can be decided on the basis of my narrative.

The second characteristic that makes these *bioi* seem remote is their moral assumptions. The answer to 'What sort of man was he?' involves an evaluation of vices and virtues, as shown in the mind's control of passion within and the whole man's emotional reaction to what besets him from without. We are expected to allocate praise and blame. Without this the enterprise would be pointless. But of course the moral judgments are anachronistic; we note in Plutarch that he realizes that *aretē* in Homer denoted something different from what it denotes in his own thinking (24c), and that he can excuse the savage Coriolanus on the ground that he never had the chance of acquiring Greek civilisation,[7] but we remain conscious that no real effort has been made to bring back the distinctive ways of thinking of past periods along with their colour and magnificence.

The third limitation is related to the other two. Plutarch is not concerned with his *viri illustres* as themselves decisive figures in history, with the Gracchi as the initiators of a social revolution, or with Alexander as the creator of the Hellenistic world; any interpretation of history that lays stress on the *influence* of great men, and treats events as the sum of their contributions, has no right to claim Plutarch as a patron. On the contrary, he barely notices the wider historical influence of his heroes, because his eyes are occupied with their individual human qualities. The exception proves the rule: the lawgivers, Lycurgus and Solon, Numa and Publicola, affected the future of their countries by conscious planning.

[7] *Coriolanus* 1.

The antecedents of the *Lives* have been very much discussed.[8] Plutarch is the culmination of ancient biographical writing as well as its most considerable monument. Yet, after all, he was not a writer of great originality. In the *Lives*, as in the other works, what we should look for is the felicitous assembly of inherited elements. What did he inherit and what use did he make of it? Classical historians had of course been concerned with the actions and careers of great men, and indeed with occasional evaluations of personality.[9] In the fourth century this concern became markedly more prominent. Xenophon is significant here. His portraits of the Greek generals at the end of the second book of the *Anabasis* are genuinely individualised descriptions, motivated by strong likes and dislikes. His *Agesilaus* too, where historical material is re-cast in the rhetorical mould of the encomium, was an influential model. Despite the differences of lay-out and purpose, the rhetorical encomium is relevant to the development of Plutarchan biography, because it—with its reverse, the invective (*psogos*)—gave much of the framework for the moral evaluation. More specifically, we see the influence of encomia in lives like Plutarch's *Timoleon* and *Cato the Younger*, where the principal sources were laudatory, or in the *Agricola* of Plutarch's contemporary Tacitus. Insofar as he expects us to praise and blame, Plutarch cannot help being in the tradition of this kind of epidictic rhetoric.

With the Isocrateans Ephorus and Theopompus the alliance of rhetoric and history was firmly established. Theopompus' huge and discursive work included a good deal of character-study. He devoted much space to the *bioi*, the life-styles, of particular groups or individuals like the courtiers and boon-companions of Philip or the Athenian *dēmagogoi*. A later Greek critic[10] regards him as a master in revealing the mysteries of the human heart, exposing dissembling virtue and unmasking concealed vice. The fragments

[8] See F. W. Walbank, Oxford Classical Dictionary[2], s.v. Biography, Greek; D. R. Stuart, *Epochs of Greek and Roman Biography*, 1928. A. Momigliano, *The Development of Greek Biography*, 1972, makes a fresh appraisal of the problems, which I have not been able to take account of here.

[9] e.g. Thucydides 1.138 on Themistocles.   [10] Dionysius, *Ad Pompeium* 12.

hardly bear this out; what passed for perspicacity looks more like commonplace invective and unsupported innuendo. Theopompus crudely anticipates the stately malice of a Tacitus. Plutarch, who disliked the attribution of unworthy motives, can have had little sympathy with him.

It was in fourth-century Athens that were formed the patterns of intellectual life that dominated Greco-Roman literature from that time forward. This was the age in which the two rival educations, philosophy and rhetoric, competed and compromised. We have seen something of the impact of rhetoric on the development of biography. The contribution of philosophy was even more decisive. It begins with the pupils of Socrates, whose portrayal of their master gives us the first delineation of a great man whose activity and personality are seen as an integral whole. The oddities of Socrates' behaviour are not simply curiosities; they are bound up with his mission of teaching and questioning. Two generations after Socrates came the development of a detailed ethical and psychological theory in the work of Aristotle and his successors. Without the *Ethics*, there would have been no such thing as Plutarchan biography. All the basic assumptions are here. A man must live with his inherited nature (*phusis*), but he may habituate (*ethizein*) and train his moral character (*ēthos*); excellence (*aretē*) is to be found in a just and balanced reaction to stimulus and emotion. Aristotle's account of the particular virtues can often be illustrated by examples out of the *Lives*. The Peripatos, however, made another contribution, perhaps even more important. It respected fact. Aristotle himself undertook an enormous amount of collecting and arranging of facts of social and political history, on much the same principles as in his biological work. But in ethics, it seems to have been his successor Theophrastus who supplied the collection of observations. Theophrastus' ethical works were full of examples. We see from his *Characters* that he had a sharp eye for diagnostic trivia. We know from Plutarch that he discussed a question central to the biographer's problem, namely to what extent a man's nature (*phusis*) could change.[11] It is the

[11] *Pericles* 38.

loss of his works that makes the most serious gap in our knowledge of Plutarch's antecedents.

The theories and researches of the philosophers thus made moral biography possible. At the same time they limited its progress. Individuals could all too easily be regarded simply as examples of emotions or virtues. Plutarch himself does not always succeed in avoiding this simplification. His heroes tend to be representative figures, in whom one set of qualities is dominant and everything else that can be said of them is made to seem marginal. Often it is ambition (*philotimia*) that takes the centre of the stage, but there are many variations: *Cimon* is a sermon on the use of wealth, *Coriolanus* on anger, *Pyrrhus* on 'always wanting more', *Antony* on the dangers of love, and so on.

It is perhaps wisest to renounce the attempt to construct a history of biographical writing in Hellenistic times. Public men, an Aratus or a Philopoemen, wrote memoirs; scholars and popularisers wrote 'lives' of literary men or philosophers. Neither genre is very close to the moral biography of a Plutarch though the memoirs of statesmen are among his most fruitful sources. The best known Hellenistic biography, Satyrus' *Euripides*, is far removed from anything of the sort. Written as a dialogue, it quotes largely from the plays to extract opinions on all kinds of subjects; it tries also to trace connections of influence between the philosophers and Euripides and again between Euripides and the writers of New Comedy who followed him. So far as any extant remains go, there is nothing here to show whence Plutarch may have taken the 'laws' of his genre.

However, monographs on the lives of great men obviously existed in Hellenistic times. There survives a Latin adaptation of the form: the *Viri Illustres* by Cornelius Nepos, the learned friend to whom Catullus dedicated his *lepidum libellum*. These brief narratives presuppose not only the habit of excerpting historians, but a tradition of the portrayal of character. And twelve of Nepos' twenty-three 'famous generals of foreign nations' are among Plutarch's subjects.

Now there is reason to think that Plutarch knew some of

Nepos' works, and used him for Roman history.[12] Perhaps the simple style was an attraction to a foreign reader. But that he used him for the story of Pelopidas or Alcibiades seems a very remote possibility. The similarities between the two lives of Alcibiades are therefore evidence of a common source. The tradition was exceptionally rich. This, as Plutarch recognised, was due to the Socratic connection. This is why we even know the names of Alcibiades' wet-nurse and *paidagōgos*, whereas with other great Athenians of the day, like Alcibiades' colleagues Nicias and Demosthenes, the other commanders in Sicily, not even the mother's name is on record.[13] There was a mass of information and opinion, contemporary or nearly so. The richness is reflected even in Nepos. In his opening paragraph, Alcibiades is presented to the Roman reader—Nepos is an apologist of Hellenic things— as a wonder of nature, possessed of all the virtues and, in his hours of relaxation, all the vices. There follows (2) a chapter on connections with Pericles, Hipponicus and Socrates. Alcibiades' *amores* need a special apology, for the Romans regarded homosexuality as a repugnant Greek vice. From this, Nepos jumps to the Sicilian expedition and the matter of the Hermae and the mysteries. The sequels to all this, the condemnation, the exile and the triumphal return, are related with some fullness (3–6). At the point of greatest success, when Alcibiades' goods have been restored and the curses on him revoked, comes the warning of sudden change: 'This happiness did not last so very long' (7.1). Alcibiades' immense reputation itself leads to his downfall, because —and this is a point Plutarch also makes (35.2)—people simply could not believe that so able a man could be liable to accidental error; when things went wrong, he must have intended it. Hence the second exile. A fairly full narrative of the latter years (7–10) is rounded off (11) by a general summary. According to this, the historians Thucydides, Timaeus and Theopompus all praised him, and in particular emphasised his versatility: all things to all men, he lived ascetically with the Spartans, drank with the Thracians, indulged with the Persians.

[12] *Marcellus* 30, *Ti. Gracchus* 21, *Lucullus* 43. [13] Plutarch, *Alcibiades* 1.

This is on a smaller scale than Plutarch's Life, and of course much more elementary. Plutarch both incorporates more historical fact (it would be impossible for him to leave out the earlier part of Alcibiades' political career, even though he found it difficult to be precise about its stages) and assumes an altogether different order of knowledge in his readers. Nevertheless, the main pattern is the same; inevitably, the successes and reverses come when they do. One thing strikes one at once: Plutarch's different placing of the two inherited general *topoi*. The theme of *anōmalia*, the discrepancy between Alcibiades' public and private life, was placed by Nepos at the beginning, as an eye-catching prooemium. In Plutarch (16), it comes at a crucial point in the narrative—or rather, just before a true continuous narrative begins, in other words on the eve of the Sicilian expedition. Its function is to explain what Alcibiades' standing was at this juncture. It is documented, with characteristic care, out of comedy and oratory. The second general topic, that of versatility, which we happen to know to have been treated very similarly by Satyrus,[14] is also placed with care (23). It comes at the moment of the first exile, when Alcibiades first showed how he could adapt to changed circumstances. Plutarch's chameleon-like Alcibiades has of course a more moral tinge than in Nepos; he is recognisably the exemplary *kolax*.[15] Nepos indeed makes no moral judgment. For him, Alcibiades is merely a great man of remarkable qualities. Plutarch appears to have selected C. Marcius Coriolanus and Alcibiades, like Demetrius and Antony,[16] as deterrent examples. This probably means that they are late in the series, and it is clear enough that they are products of his mature skill. The placing of these *topoi* evinces this as plainly as anything.[17]

Before he began the 'parallels', Plutarch seems to have written a few other lives, notably those of the Caesars, of which *Galba* and *Otho* survive. This series did not include the Flavians. It may therefore have been completed before 96, and if that is so is almost certainly earlier than any of the others. The tone and the discus-

---

[14] Athenaeus 12.534B.
[16] See below, p. 135.
[15] See above, p. 95.
[17] See below, pp. 122 ff.

sion of method are however very similar,[18] and there is not enough in what survives to justify an attempt to see here an earlier stage of Plutarch's art.[19] In any case, it is the 'parallels' that matter. There can be little doubt that they were meant from the first as an extensive series, though presumably it grew under the hand and there was no initial overall plan. The idea of drawing parallels between Roman and Greek (or other non-Roman) achievements was naturally not new. It is present in Nepos, it gives the structure of Valerius Maximus' vast collection of *exempla*, which Plutarch knew and apparently used. A comparison of Themistocles with Coriolanus seems to have been drawn by Atticus.[20] But it is easy to believe that Plutarch had the contemporary situation in mind. In *The Glory of Athens*, he had argued the case that Athenian achievement could rival Rome even in the practical sphere. The 'parallels' offer a larger demonstration of the same point. There was a topicality in all this in an age when Greek senators and consuls were becoming commoner. If Sosius himself was a Greek,[21] the dedication had a particular aptness. In such a situation, Greece might seem to have a special contribution to make to world affairs: a civilisation and humanity which the *ferus victor* had sometimes lacked. To say that Plutarch may have felt this is not to think of him as in any sense anti-Roman. That would be absurd. Nor is he making a conscious effort to build a bridge between alien cultures; he did not see them as alien. It is enough to point out that the scheme of parallels possesses a certain appeal at this juncture which it did not have before. An important sector of Plutarch's readers consisted of Greek speakers called to imperial office; he seeks to give them an ideal, to indicate the spirit in which they should accept the challenge.

But the political appeal of the scheme of 'parallels' is not of course its most significant feature. It also gave Plutarch a new

[18] Note *Galba* 1, 3.2.
[19] *Galba* and *Otho* however are not independent narratives; such interlocking is natural in a series, and we see something of the same technique in the *Gracchi* and in *Agis and Cleomenes*.
[20] Cicero, *Brutus* 43.
[21] Above, p. 10.

kind of interest in the consideration of character. Without it, his kind of 'moral biography' would perhaps hardly have been possible.

Of the extant pairs of *Lives*, all but four have formal 'comparisons' (*sunkriseis*) appended. There seems no valid reason why Plutarch should not have written them for these four also; they may well have been lost.[22] The comparisons do not make very attractive reading. They add little to the information contained in the narrative. They are, as it were, model answers for a rhetorical exercise: you have heard the two stories, what points of similarity and difference can you see? Such things were of course practised in the schools. Quintilian (2.4.21) gives two advanced exercises which can be used to stimulate progress when simple *narratio* has been mastered. One consists of encomium and invective (*laudare claros viros et vituperare improbos*). This exercises the mind with varied material, trains the moral instincts and lays in a store of *exempla* which will be useful to the orator one day. The other exercise is comparison—'Which is the better man and which the worse?' This gives double the amount of material to handle and deals not only with the nature of virtues and vices but with the degree (*modus*) in which they are present. Plutarch's *sunkriseis* are specimens of this kind of work.

The comparison of Alcibiades with Coriolanus is a good example.

We have now set out all the actions (*praxeis*) that we regard as worth mentioning and recording (*logou kai mnēmēs axias*). It is evident that their actions in war show no decisive difference in favour of either party. Both alike exhibited many acts of soldierly daring and courage, and in their commands many acts of skill and forethought. One might perhaps adjudge Alcibiades the more perfect general, because he was consistently victorious and successful both by land and by sea. Both shared the characteristic of manifestly giving success to their own side by their presence and generalship and even more manifestly damaging it by their desertion. As to their political life, Alcibiades' pretentious style, with the tastelessness and vulgarity that came from his playing

[22] But see H. Erbse, *Hermes* 1956, 398 ff.

to the mob, disgusted decent folk; while Marcius' totally graceless, overweening and oligarchical manner earned the hatred of the Roman people (*dēmos*). Neither is to be commended. However, blame attaches less to the favour-seeking demagogue than to politicians who insult the common people in order not to be thought demagogues. To flatter the *dēmos* for power is disgraceful; to win power by terrorizing, violence and oppression is not only disgraceful (*aischron*), it is wrong (*adikon*). (1)

This judgment is characteristic in many ways. It is orderly: military exploits are considered apart from political, and within the sphere of the military 'soldierlike' qualities are distinguished from generalship. One thinks of Homer's

> both good king and valiant spearman.[23]

The key to the political judgment is the treatment of the *dēmos*; no historical differences between the Athenians of the fifth century and the Roman plebs of the fifth century are apparently admitted. And the bias of the opinion is in Alcibiades' favour. This is because, though Plutarch inherited from Plato and other older literature an anti-democratic model of politics, this was less important to him than the criteria of humane and fair dealing against which Coriolanus offended so conspicuously. Moreover, there was for him a distinct association between the humane and the democratic.

Both these characters, let us remember, are in the last resort blameworthy.

It is plain that Marcius is regarded as simple and straightforward (*authekastos*: an Aristotelian term for a man who calls a spade a spade) in his ways (*tropos*), and Alcibiades as politically dishonest (*panourgos*) and insincere. The most serious accusation of malice and deceitfulness against the latter relates to his cheating the Spartan ambassadors and so destroying the peace, as Thucydides tells us. This policy however, though it involved the city in war again, made it strong and formidable by the acquisition, through Alcibiades, of the Mantinean and Argive alliances. But we are told of Marcius by Dionysius that he

[23] *Iliad* 3.179.

stirred up war between Romans and Volscians by a trick, falsely accusing the visitors to the games. The motive makes this the baser act. Marcius was not moved, like Alcibiades, by ambition or political conflict, but gave way to his anger—from which, says Dion,[24] no one gets thanks—and so threw many areas of Italy into confusion, and incidentally sacrificed many innocent cities to his anger against his country. Alcibiades, it is true, caused his countrymen many disasters through anger. But as soon as he saw them repent, he forgave them, and, when he was thrown out a second time, he felt no glee at the generals' mistakes and did not let them run into danger through bad advice. He acted in fact in the way in which Aristides is particularly praised for acting towards Themistocles . . . Marcius on the other hand (*i*) damaged the whole community, though only a section of it had done him harm and the best and highest elements shared his injuries and his sufferings; (*ii*) remained unmoved and unyielding in spite of many deputations and requests trying to assuage his sole anger and folly, and made it plain that he had undertaken a cruel and remorseless war not to win his country back and return from exile but to destroy it and cast it down . . . (2.1–2.7)

Here again, it is Coriolanus who comes off worse. Plutarch is even willing to use as an argument the statement of Dionysius about his treacherous behaviour to the Volscians which he at least hesitated over in the *Life* itself.[25] The chief criterion is reaction to injury. Alcibiades forgives and puts his country first. This line is followed also in the discussion (5) of Coriolanus' final surrender to his mother's entreaties. He thought more of a mere woman than of his country! Granted that one may quite properly choose not to 'pay court to the mob', Coriolanus failed to accept the consequences of his policy, as wiser and better men—Metellus, Aristides, Epaminondas, all of whom are subjects of Lives—had done.

There is thus a clear condemnation of Coriolanus for the moral attitudes of his public life. But the balance is not all on that side:

[24] 'Dion' may be the Syracusan statesman whose life Plutarch wrote, but this is uncertain. For the sentiment, cf. Menander fr. 516 Körte: 'No one wins thanks from anger'.

[25] 26.3. 'Some say' in this passage means Dionysius; it is not uncommon for Plutarch to refer to a single authority in some such vague phrase.

These are all the faults one can find with him. Everything else was brilliant. For temperance (*sōphrosunē*) and continence with money he may properly be compared to the best and purest of the Greeks—certainly not to Alcibiades, who was utterly outrageous in this and quite without thought of honour. (5)

The *sunkriseis* are thus an essential part of the plan of 'parallels'. How the pairs were chosen, and how the plan developed, must remain largely uncertain. It had begun with Epaminondas, Plutarch's Boeotian philosopher-hero, celebrated also in *Socrates' Sign*. This Life is lost, as is its pair—a Scipio, more probably Africanus than Aemilianus.[26] Beyond this, we know certain fixed points: *Demosthenes* and *Cicero* formed Book Five, *Pericles* and *Fabius* Book Ten, and *Dion* and *Brutus* Book Twelve. Most of the gaps in the first twelve pairs can be fairly plausibly filled; but the cross-references which are used to determine the order of the whole series give a confusing and in places inconsistent picture.[27] Something however can be observed about the actual choice of parallels. When *Numa* had been written, Plutarch resolved to push back his Roman researches to Romulus, on whom he had doubtless now done the reading; to set against him, he introduced Theseus, going (as he puts it) beyond the bounds of history to a region of time as remote as the 'Scythian frost' and 'frozen sea' that geographers put on the edges of the world-map.[28] Solon was a desirable subject; to parallel him, Plutarch thought of Publicola, though the material was obviously thin. The desire to include the Gracchi brought in Agis and Cleomenes. Lucullus was recommended by certain personal connections with Chaeronea; Cimon, also distinguished for his wealth and generosity, seemed a possible companion. Sertorius was selected before his parallel Eumenes. Thus it is sometimes the Greek and

[26] Appian, *Syriaca* 41, makes a comparison between Africanus and Epaminondas in regard to their reactions to accusation and trial. This sounds very Plutarchan, as Hirzel thought. Further, in selecting a parallel for his special hero, Plutarch will have aimed high: so the conqueror of Hannibal suits better.
[27] They are studied in detail by Stoltz (above, p. 101, n. 4).
[28] *Theseus* 1.

sometimes the Roman who came to mind first. The grounds of comparison also vary, and are sometimes not the most obvious. Thus with Cicero and Demosthenes, Plutarch makes the point that it is not only as the greatest orators that he couples them, but also (and more significantly) because their careers showed common features (exile, death of a daughter) and their personalities common characteristics (political vigour, disinclination for war). But why were Lysander and Sulla paired? Both indeed were generals, both were self-made. But the comparison shows more differences than likenesses, differences which are typical of the contrast between Greece and Rome: Lysander wins the prize for self-control and moderation (*enkrateia, sōphrosunē*), Sulla for courage and generalship. Perhaps the last item in the list gives a clue:

Finally, their behaviour regarding Athens has some weight in the comparison of their characters. Sulla captured the city when it had gone to war against him on behalf of Mithridates' power and hegemony; nevertheless he left it free and independent. Lysander, at the moment of Athens' loss of hegemony and empire, took no pity on her; he took away the democracy and gave her the cruellest and most lawless of tyrants. (43.5)

Paradoxical as this is in the light of the overall judgment, it makes an interesting point: 'liberating Hellas' ranks very high, if it can redeem a Sulla or a Nero. In short, either character or circumstance may be the basis of a *sunkrisis*; similar events affecting dissimilar persons and similar persons reacting to contrasting events alike provide a suitable field for the exercise. It is basically a rhetorical procedure; but it is rescued from the implausibilities of purely rhetorical ingenuity by its value as a way of concentrating and directing the moral reflections which are the primary purpose of biography.

The formality of the *sunkriseis* leads us to expect some formality too in the Lives. There are indeed recurrent themes and elements. There is very often an elaborate preface, leading into the subject with a sophisticated play of analogy, and raising such methodological issues as the difference between history and biography or the moral value of historical studies. Family, education, personal appearance are regular topics of the opening chapters. We see how the child displays the coming man, or how some special circumstances, like being orphaned,[29] both reveals nature and affects the future.

The début in public and military life is signalised, and thereafter the narrative seems to be so shaped as to throw into relief certain moments of success and to show how success often turns to failure through mismanagement, bad luck or (easiest of all) the almost automatic envy (*phthonos*) of the less successful. In some Lives, shape is also given to the story by a kind of internal *sunkrisis* with conflicting personalities; the cautious Fabius Maximus is contrasted successively with five other Roman generals, of whom three meet disaster through imprudence, the fourth (Marcellus) proves a good colleague, and the last (Scipio) outshines the hero himself.[30]

That the hinges of a Life, as it were, are major *events* must not make us lose sight of the fact that its main purpose is not narrative but description and evaluation. There is of course the linear movement from birth to death, and careers are divided into more or less distinct periods. But within these periods, and to some extent in the whole as well, the considerations that determine arrangement are those of character and subject, rather than date. There are consequently many passages where no clear chronology can be seen. This has sometimes misled readers. It has also given rise to the theory that Plutarch consciously combined two different types of writing, the 'eidological'—roughly, 'descriptive'—and the 'chronographic'.[31] This theory served to discourage naïve historical interpretations, but on the whole it darkens counsel; it is truer to say that there are in fact no 'chronographic' parts, except indeed for the occasional résumé which Plutarch needs to connect episodes. This is usually brief, and

[29] Coriolanus, Philopoemen.
[30] See my remarks, *Greece and Rome* 1966, 150 f.
[31] A. Weiszäcker, *Untersuchungen über Plutarchs biographische Technik*, 1931.

assumes a general knowledge of the period in the reader. It is written to remind rather than to inform.

The *Lives* thus give an impression of being written not indeed to a precise formula, but within a fairly well defined pattern. At the same time there are very marked differences of treatment and style between one Life and another. These are mainly due to differences in the nature of the raw material. Sometimes Plutarch makes it clear that he is aware of a special problem. Rigorous selectivity was needed in *Alexander* and *Caesar*. In *Nicias*, Thucydides could be taken as read and there was no sense in rivalling him. Aristides and Pelopidas were both persons who played a subordinate part in great events in which others took the lead; Plutarch exaggerates their personal rôle. The lives of the lawgivers are naturally more static, and their legislation is seen as part of the evidence for their moral qualities. The Hellenistic historians on whom *Pyrrhus* and *Demetrius* depend emphasised the vicissitudes of fortune and the drama of events; these Lives are full of reversals and melodrama. *Sertorius* appears to be based largely on Sallust. Its military narrative has an unusual conciseness, which it is tempting to think of as a reflection of Sallustian *brevitas*. But Plutarch's relation to his sources is complex and varied. He wrote from a retentive memory of vast reading and almost every word he used was loaded with allusion. This holds for the *Lives* as well as for the *Moralia*. And it is this that makes interpretation difficult. Plutarch's evocation of the past is both factual and linguistic. Its nature can hardly be seen except in detail; and the work of commenting on him, though it has been long pursued, has in some senses hardly begun.

CHAPTER SEVEN

Alcibiades, or The Flatterer: an analysis

In any study of the *Lives*, detailed analysis of content is an essential stage. We have already seen something of *Alcibiades*; it is worth while developing this a little as an example.[1] We saw that the abundant and varied tradition gave opportunities here which were not common in subjects from Greek history. Plutarch used them, not to give a fuller narrative than usual, but to give an unusually elaborate interpretation of character. In his own words:

Alcibiades' *ēthos* subsequently, as was to be expected (*eikos*) amid great events and changing fortunes, displayed many internal discrepancies and variations. By nature (*phusei*) however, while he possessed many important emotional tendencies (*pathē*), it was the love of winning and of taking the first place that was the strongest. The sayings of his childhood make this clear. (2.1)

The distinction between the permanent endowment (*phusis*) and the acquired characteristics of *ēthos* is here unusually plain. In the course of the Life, Plutarch is going to make it clear that the changes in Alcibiades' *ēthos* were not only superficial but to a large extent deliberate. This is why he is more unambiguous about the *phusis-ēthos* distinction here than in some other Lives. But all this is later. For the moment, we have the child Alcibiades before us.

[1] I have dealt with some of the material in more detail, *Proceedings of the Cambridge Philological Society*, 1966, 37 ff.

The arrangement even of these first anecdotes illustrates clearly the principles on which Plutarch groups his material. Chronological considerations are subordinated to thematic. The first group of stories relates to education and play: Alcibiades bites his wrestling partner (2.2), lies down in the street when a cart threatens to run over the knuckle-bones he is playing with (2.3–4), and refuses to distort his face by learning to play the *aulos*[2]—with the consequence that it goes completely out of fashion (2.5–7). The chronological indications in this chapter—'while still small' (2.3) and 'when he came to learning' (2.5)[3]—give what Plutarch infers to be the sequence of these two events. It is a misinterpretation to suppose that they tell us anything more—for example, that the wrestling episode preceded the game in the street (which seems unlikely), or that what follows in 3.1, where Alcibiades 'as a boy' runs away from his guardian's house, is necessarily subsequent in time to all the anecdotes so far related. The runaway episode is in fact the start of a new development, which continues to the end of chapter 6. The theme of this is Alcibiades' relations with his lovers. *Erōs*, though not a central theme of this Life as it is of *Antony*, is none the less an important topic. It is taken up in the lurid last scene (39), where Alcibiades is in the burning house with his mistress Timandra, and it is she who buries him. Within this 'erotic' section we have once again imprecise chronology, combined with a certain attempt to convey an impression of development. The runaway Alcibiades is a boy (*pais*) who already has a lover; he is a *pais* also when Socrates' attentions give proof of his remarkable qualities (*euphuia*). But the affair with Socrates of course went on for a long time; Plutarch draws, inevitably, on Plato's *Symposium*, and must have known that at its dramatic date (416 B.C.) Alcibiades was in his late thirties. And the anecdote in chapter 5, in which Alcibiades gives a guarantee on behalf of one of his lovers at a tax-auction, implies control of property, and so adulthood. Now at 7.1 there is a specific indication of the passage of time: he was 'passing beyond the years of boyhood' when he

---

[2] A wind instrument: 'flute' in the common translation; 'clarinet' may be more accurate.   [3] cf. *Cato the Younger* 1.6.

encountered the regrettable schoolmaster who had no copy of Homer and that other schoolmaster who had one 'corrected by himself' and whose superior learning was wasted on children, because 'he ought to be educating the young men (*neoi*)'. The last half of this story evidently presupposes that Alcibiades is himself a 'young man'. Now the other extant versions know nothing of this second schoolmaster. Yet it seems unlikely that Plutarch invented him. Probably he found him in the tradition, and then used him as an indication of the date of the entire episode. Immediately after this comes a story (7.3) in which Alcibiades recommends a very worried Pericles to look for ways, not of rendering his accounts to the *dēmos*, but of not rendering them. This time, other versions[4] describe Alcibiades as *pais* or *puer*. Plutarch does not. Does he, we may wonder, wish us to place this too as a story of adolescence? Did the sarcastic wit strike him as beyond the powers of a young boy?

The next new beginning is at 7.3. 'While he was still a lad (*meirakion*)', Alcibiades fought at Potidaea. True: in 432/1 he was in his early twenties. So at first sight this looks like a stage forward chronologically. In fact, it is not this, but the introduction to a new topic, namely Alcibiades' personal bravery. This, like *erōs*, has its importance as a motif in the subsequent narrative. It is exemplified here by Potidaea and by his bravery at Delium, eight years later. Both campaigns are mentioned in one of Plutarch's primary sources, Plato's *Symposium*. It was natural that he should keep them together.

After bravery, self-assurance; for this seems to be the link between the stories in chapters 8 and 9, in which Alcibiades acts with notable disregard for public opinion. Though Plutarch excuses, at least to some extent, the high-handed response to his wife's desertion (8.5), it is plain that the tendency of all these stories is unfavourable. Alcibiades, we see, possessed not only courage, which is a virtue, but its vicious counterpart, audacity.[5]

---

[4] Diodorus 12.38; Valerius Maximus 3.1. ext. 1.
[5] cf. Aristotle, *Nicomachean Ethics* 2.8, on courage (*andreia*) as a mean between the opposing vicious extremes of *thrasutēs* (audacity) and *deilia* (cowardice).

The whole of the first nine chapters deals with moral qualities in the setting of private life. Alcibiades is a citizen, not yet a politician. In 10, we pass to the political début, a point Plutarch often signalises. At first sight, there seems to be a sort of chronological sequence: 'first approach' to public life in 10.1, 'the doors opened wide' to a political career in 10.3. But it is wrong to read it like this. The link is again a thematic one, the theme being Alcibiades' advantages for public life. In 10.1–2, we are shown how he first gained the affection of the *dēmos*, on the day when, after generously promising an unsolicited contribution to public funds, he let his pet quail escape from his clothes and the whole *ekklēsia* got up and tried to catch it. The episode suggests a scene of comedy; it seems to be in effect a note on a personality, Antiochus, Alcibiades' life-long protégé and assistant. Annotations of comedy frequently took this form.[6] From 10.3 to 12.3 runs a more connected development. Alcibiades' chief advantages were his oratory, on which he prided himself, and his wealth, which enabled him to compete at Olympia. All this is plainly description rather than chronological narrative, and much of it, once again, is attached to pieces of literary history: the victory-hymn by Euripides, the speech of Isocrates *On the Chariot* (11.3, 12.3). It is well to be reminded that a good deal of ancient historical knowledge crystallised round the interpretation of texts.

13.1 again looks like the start of a narrative:

When he entered the political arena, still a mere lad (*meirakion*), he at once humiliated all the other *dēmagōgoi*, but had a struggle with Phaeax and Nicias . . .

But, unless the upper age-limit for a *meirakion* can be taken to be about thirty-five, which is unlikely, the phrase 'at once' conceals an uncomfortably long interval, for the situation in which Phaeax and Nicias were Alcibiades' rivals is the one which came to a head in the ostracism of Hyperbolus in 417.

This episode itself follows directly (13.4–9). Plutarch had already handled it in *Nicias* (11), and the comparison affords a

[6] cf. W. von Uxkull-Gyllenband, *Plutarch und die griechische Biographie*, 17 ff.

good example of the differences that follow from the different points of view the biographer adopts for the purposes of particular Lives. (*i*) We observe, for example, the different choice of terms of disapproval for the unhappy Hyperbolus. In *Nicias* he is

a man with no influence to give him daring, but advancing by his daring to influence, a disrepute to the city because of the repute he had in it. He thought himself far from the risk of ostracism, being to be sure better suited to the pillory . . .

In *Alcibiades*:

Even Thucydides[7] mentions him as a bad character, and he provided almost all the comic poets with a topic for stage-jokes. Untroubled and undisturbed as he was by hard words, because of his total disregard for reputation—a sort of shamelessness that some people call confidence and courage—no one liked him, though the *dēmos* often employed him when it wanted to blacken or disgrace men of better standing . . .

Minor characters in the *Lives* are often conceived in terms of a comparison with the hero. This may well be so here. Nicias had every *aretē*: status, wealth, integrity, courage. Hyperbolus is a plain contrast; the blackest terms are appropriate. Between Alcibiades and Hyperbolus, on the other hand, there is a more complex comparative relationship. Disregard for public opinion, is, as we have seen, one of Alcibiades' own features; but it is present in Hyperbolus without the backing of status and origin which might make it excusable. (*ii*) The narrative itself also shows a difference, and a significant one. In *Alcibiades*, it is Alcibiades who takes the initiative in bringing his faction and Nicias' together against Hyperbolus; in *Nicias*, the initiative is a joint one. (*iii*) Finally, the variant version according to which it was Phaeax with whom Alcibiades intrigued receives a bare mention in *Nicias*, though its authority, Theophrastus, is named. In *Alcibiades*— where incidentally Theophrastus' name does not appear—it is given in more detail. If it really was Phaeax, the story has no relevance to Nicias' career, though it has for that of Alcibiades.

This episode, like the preceding ones, is not to be thought of as

[7] 'Even' because Thucydides is conspicuously free from malice.

part of a continuous narrative. It places Alcibiades in conflict with Nicias for the first time, and it leads up to chapter 14, where the conflict is seen in terms of foreign policy; in this round, Alcibiades prevails, and chapter 15 is devoted to his successful overseas achievements. The events are not in order. The episode of the Long Walls of Patrae (15.6) belongs to 419, whereas what immediately precedes it happened two years later.

Thus everything so far—and we are nearly halfway through the Life—may be regarded as generalised description, with a broad but not exact chronological progression, and thematic grouping of many details. This method reaches a climax in the lavish embellishment and documentation of the *anōmalia* theme which occupies chapter 16:

Amid all this high policy and oratory, this pride and intelligence, there was much of another sort to be seen: luxurious living, outrages of drink and lust, the effeminate purple clothes trailing through the *agora*; monstrous extravagance; decks of triremes sawn away to enable the bedding to be slung on straps and not rest on bare boards, so that Alcibiades should sleep softer; the gilded shield with its Eros bearing a thunderbolt, instead of one of the traditional devices. Seeing all this made the notables not only disgusted and angry but frightened of his high-handedness and lawlessness, as alien and tyrannical, while the attitude of the *dēmos* is well expressed by Aristophanes in the line:

Longs for him, hates him, and so much wants to have him . . .[8]

One day, when Alcibiades had done well and was being escorted out of the *ekklēsia* with great *éclat*, the misanthrope Timon[9] met him; and instead of avoiding him, as he did everyone else, he went up and clasped him by the hand. 'You're growing up nicely, lad,' he said; 'you are growing into a mighty misfortune for all these people.' Some laughed, some cursed, some were a good deal disturbed by the remark. So indeterminate was the reputation that Alcibiades had acquired because of the inconsistencies of his nature.

This *locus*, which we saw in Nepos and most of which goes back

---

[8] *Frogs* 1422—written in 405, ten or more years after the events narrated here. Plutarch no doubt knew this, but clearly thinks the anachronism is of no significance.

[9] cf. *Antony* 70.3.

at least to Satyrus, and probably to fourth-century sources, is clearly in origin a comment on the whole career. Plutarch's originality shows itself in two ways: in the working up of the passage, and in its placing. By putting it here, he emphasises at a crucial point that we have to do, not with a potential saviour, but with a brilliant enigma. The first word of the next chapter is ominous, and the order is chosen for effect: 'Sicily . . .'

The 'anomaly' passage and the similarly elaborate 'chameleon' *locus* of 23 are like two choruses in a tragedy. This is an obvious and close analogy, though it would be a hazardous operation to extend it or to look for 'dramatic' structure in the *Lives* in general. The *epeisodion* which divides our two passages comprises the narrative of the Sicilian expedition, embracing also the affairs of the Hermae and the mysteries. This central topic of Athenian history is naturally related from Alcibiades' angle. We should observe particularly the motivations in 21.7–8. The punishment of those whom Andocides had denounced did not satiate the anger of the *dēmos*. It still had resentment to spare. Yet it was unhappy about recalling Alcibiades, because he could so easily make the army mutiny, and to leave Nicias in command offered a poor prospect of rapid success. The point of this is to emphasise yet again that, whatever else was in question about Alcibiades, his ability was beyond doubt.

The second 'chorus' (23) takes the revelation of Alcibiades' character a stage further. What had seemed, in the context of Athenian politics and society, erratic and unpredictable brilliance, is now seen to be a capacity for infinite changes of style to suit changed circumstances. This very appropriately comes at the point where Alcibiades first needs the versatility of the successful refugee. As in 16, Plutarch begins (23.3) by relating private qualities to public activity:

While he enjoyed public repute and admiration, he was also wooing the mass of the people in private ways, enchanting them with his Spartan style of life. Seeing him with his hair cut short, taking cold baths, eating plain bread and drinking black broth,[10] they could hardly

[10] Traditional Spartan fare, and apparently an acquired taste.

believe that he had ever had a cook in his house, or set eyes on a perfumer, or could bear so much as the touch of a cloak of Milesian wool. It was, they say, one of his many ingenious methods of captivating people, to be able to assimilate himself and share intimately in their habits and ways of life. He could change quicker than the chameleon. Indeed, there is one colour, or so they say, that that animal is incapable of simulating, namely, white; but Alcibiades found nothing anywhere, good or bad, that he was unable to reproduce and put into practice. Athletic, plain-living and grim-faced in Sparta, he was luxurious, charming and easy-going in Ionia, while in Thrace he devoted himself to drinking and riding. When he visited the satrap Tissaphernes, his splendour and extravagance surpassed Persian standards of magnificence. It was not that he could shift from one personality (*tropos*) to another all that easily, or that his character (*ēthos*) admitted every conceivable change. It was rather that when he found that it would offend the company to behave according to his own nature (*phusis*), he would conceal it and take refuge in any form or fashion that suited the moment.

Plutarch here reveals what he takes to be the central truth about his 'hero': the changes (*metabolai*) were deliberate, the versatility that of the *kolax*[11] This is how the subsequent successes were won; this is how an Athenian aristocrat, not in the least dependent on being within sight and sound of the Pnyx, contrived to make a new career wherever fortune took him.

Like all success, this very personal achievement lay open to the attack of malice. We see this almost at once, in the jealousy (*phthonos*) of the Spartan notables (24.3). Alcibiades has to flee to the wily intriguer Tissaphernes—an episode alluded to already in the 'chorus' (23.5).

The military and political history of all this period is involved and complex. Plutarch naturally abridges very much. He not only tells it from Alcibiades' standpoint, he exaggerates his hero's part. A good example of this is the way in which Alcibiades is made indirectly responsible for the establishment of the Four Hundred (26.1) through the activities of his friends. It is a story of sordid intrigue; yet even here Plutarch characteristically looks for great

[11] cf. above, pp. 95 ff.

qualities. If the hero is no saviour or exemplar of virtue, neither is he without some true greatness. When the democrats at Samos have raised Alcibiades to the command, he does not just let things take their course as lesser men might have done, and give way to his benefactors. He behaves with independence as well as strategic sense, and checks the rash move on Athens. This firmness contributes to a phase of rising success which continues till after the naval victory in the Hellespont late in 411 (27.6). Then comes a sudden reverse. Ambitious—*philotimoumenos*, a key word—to display his success to Tissaphernes, he repairs with gifts and a princely retinue to the satrap's presence. But Tissaphernes has other thoughts. The Spartans have found fault with him and are making things awkward at the royal court. Historians usually see these moves in rational and strategic terms: the Athenian victory had upset the balance of power on the Hellespont, and Persian policy was not to allow either of the Greek belligerents to preponderate. This is not the kind of interpretation to attract Plutarch. He sees it all rather in terms of personal influences and anxieties. Anyway, Alcibiades is a timely victim, and Tissaphernes locks him up at Sardis.

But not for long. The resourceful hero 'provides himself with a horse from somewhere'. In 'provides himself' (*euporēsas*) we recognise an Attic phrase from Xenophon's account of these events (*Hellenica* 1.1.10), but Plutarch omits much; and, to concentrate attention on the hero, he leaves out his companion Mantitheos. The escape is successful, and Alcibiades lets it be thought, to Tissaphernes' embarrassment, that it was effected with the satrap's collusion. He thus wins another round in this secondary battle of wits, which is one of the recurrent themes of the Life. There is a very similar motif in *Lysander* (especially 20), where the great Spartan intriguer clashes with the other satrap, Pharnabazus. The Greeks liked battles of wits: 'the fox knows many tricks, the porcupine knows one—but a big one.'[12]

In the following narratives of the campaigns in which Alcibiades commanded the Athenian forces, another recurrent theme

[12] Archilochus fr. 103 Diehl (201 West).

is highlighted. His personal bravery had been exemplified in the Socratic episodes of Potidaea and Delium. It is now illustrated by the risks he took at Selymbria (30.7). In what follows, however, the narrative becomes more discursive. Why is so much space spent on the siege of Byzantium and its sequel (31)? Not because of any particular relevance to Alcibiades, but because Plutarch is attracted by the moral problem incidentally involved. Anaxilaos, the Spartan commander who had surrendered, was subsequently tried for treason:

His defence was as honourable as his action. He said that he was not a Spartan but a Byzantine . . . and had not betrayed his city, but rescued her from war and disaster, following the example of the best of the Spartans, whose one unqualified test of the good and just (*kalon* . . . *dikaion*) was the interest of the country (*to tēs patridos sumpheron*). (31.8)

Plutarch was interested in this equation of *honestum* with *utile*; he returns to it in *Agesilaus* (37).

The rising phase now approaches a summit of success. Alcibiades' triumphant return to Athens is one of the great set-pieces of the Life:

Douris of Samos,[13] who claims descent from Alcibiades, adds that the, Pythian prizewinner Chrysogonus played the *aulos* for the rowers, and Callippides the tragic actor called the time, both wearing straight-cut tunics, long robes and full festival costume, while the admiral's ship came in under purple sails. One would think it was an evening visit after a drinking-bout! Neither Theopompus nor Ephorus nor Xenophon mentions this. Nor indeed was it likely (*eikos*) that he should so make light of the Athenians' feelings, when he was returning after exile and so many tribulations. In fact, he was apprehensive and would not disembark from the trireme on arrival until he had stood on the deck and seen that his cousin Euryptolemus and many other friends and relatives were there to welcome and encourage him.

This is a revealing passage. Plutarch loves a brilliant scene, and tries to enter into the feelings of the participants. He cannot resist

---

[13] 76F70 Jacoby, *Fr. Gr. Hist.*

Douris' detail. Yet Douris, a pupil of Theophrastus, who wrote various historical works besides the *Chronicles of Samos* from which this episode probably comes, was an unreliable authority. Plutarch's complaint against him is that he is putting forward something psychologically implausible and—worst of all— malicious. Hence the *eikos*-argument in refutation, of which this is a good instance. Whether or not the comparison of Alcibiades' behaviour with a nocturnal drinking-party is Douris' or Plutarch's is hard to say. In either case, it reflects the scene in Plato's *Symposium* where Alcibiades makes a characteristic entrance as a drunken reveller.

The brilliance of the return is soon clouded. It was ominous that the entry was on the day of the Plynteria, the annual cere-monial washing of an ancient wooden statue of Athena, when no business was normally transacted. But all seemed to go well for a time. Alcibiades' *philotimia* made him wait long enough to secure the safe passage of the initiates to Eleusis at the Mysteries. But malice soon appeared. Even this pious act was so regarded only 'by those who felt no *phthonos*'. Sinister also is Alcibiades' demagogy —another manifestation of the *kolax*—and the appeals made to him to set himself as a tyrant and

get the upper hand over *phthonos*, overthrow decrees and laws and nonsense that was ruining the city . . . and take things in hand without fear of calumniators (34.7).

So close is this passage to some of the words of Plato's Callicles in the *Gorgias* (484A, 492C) that someone, Plutarch or a source, seems to have identified Callicles, who is rather a mystery, with the historical Alcibiades.[14]

The final undoing, for which these reflections prepare us, came from a cause already hinted at (21.8): no one suffered as much as Alcibiades did from his own reputation, because no one could imagine that he could not succeed in whatever he put his hand to (35.2). The story soon moves to the point at which he leaves

---

[14] The identification has been made in modern times also, though it cannot be right.

the Athenian forces (36.5) and establishes himself in Thrace as a private war-lord, never again to command his fellow-citizens. His relation with the *polis* however are not entirely broken. When the generals at Aegospotami lay themselves open to Spartan attack, Alcibiades rides over to warn them, though in vain (36.6). This shows not only his foresight, but his magnanimity. And even when Athens has fallen, the *dēmos* still regrets its hero. Plutarch enlarges (38.2–4), on slight evidence so far as we know, but in distinctive language, on the feelings of the city:

Yet even in these circumstances some faint hope was reviving that things were not totally ruined while Alcibiades survived. 'For he was not content the previous time with the ineffective and quiet life of exile, nor will he now, if he is in a condition to do anything, suffer the Spartans to insult us and the Thirty to knock us about.'[15] It was not irrational for the mass of the people to have these dreams, when even the Thirty had anxious thoughts and were making inquiries and taking much note of what he was doing and planning.

Action follows. Critias convinces Lysander of the potential danger. Lysander, fortified by authority from home, sets the machinery of murder in motion. What motivated the Spartans? Did they really think Alcibiades' ability and ambition constituted a serious threat? Or did they simply wish to gratify Agis, whose wife he had seduced? Plutarch leaves it open; but it looks as if he inclines, once again, to the personal motive (38.6).

The death-scene itself is vividly told. There is a warning dream, in which Alcibiades imagines his mistress Timandra making up his face like a woman's. The murderers surround and set fire to the house. Alcibiades leaps out of the flames, a terrifying figure. All they dare do is to attack from a distance with spears and arrows till he falls dead. The last detail is in keeping with the whole story: Timandra buried him 'splendidly and ambitiously (*lamprōs kai philotimōs*)'.

Plutarch adds, as often, a footnote: a variant version according to which the murder was not political, but was occasioned by the

[15] *Paroinountas*, i.e. behave with drunken insolence.

private enmity of the relatives of a woman Alcibiades had seduced (39.9). This exculpates Lysander and the Spartans, and makes Alcibiades a spent wanderer, the victim not of political calculation but of his own vice. Plutarch makes no comment on the plausibility of this story, nor do we know its source. He need not have recorded it; that he did so, and chose it for his closing sentence, suggests that he means it to be retained in our minds. His moral disapproval is evident; in the comparison with Coriolanus, the worst point against Alcibiades will be his sexual licence.

Plutarch's Alcibiades is a fascinating figure, and has imposed his image on history. We see the advantages supporting that will to excel: the wealth, the oratory, the courage, the strategic intelligence. We see in even brighter light the weaknesses: the lack of *sōphrosunē* and integrity, the contempt for the moral standards of ordinary mortals. There is no doubt that the moralist condemns. Had Plutarch been writing a few years later, he might have been embarrassed, for the philhellenic emperor Hadrian had a monument erected to Alcibiades' honour at Melissa in Phrygia, the village where he was believed to have died, but which Plutarch does not name.[16]

[16] Athenaeus 574E.

CHAPTER EIGHT

Some Roman War-lords

IT is wise also to read Plutarch sometimes with the analytical eye half-closed. The analysing reader always risks forgetting what nobody else forgets: the power of description and narrative that has commanded the attention of posterity. There are examples all through the Lives, Greek as well as Roman. But the most dazzling displays are in the Roman Lives, and especially those of the *principes* of the last century of the Republic. Here was the most grandiose of subjects: the virtues and vices of the statesmen and soldiers whose careers fell in the age of tumult that was stilled by the establishment of Augustus' new order. These tumults testified, in Plutarch's view as in that of most ancient historians, to a general moral decline. That they might break out again was alarmingly demonstrated by the titanic commotions of A.D. 69.[1] The Lives of this period make up about a quarter of the whole extant collection. They have a special amplitude and elaboration. The material available about Marius and Sulla, Caesar and Pompey, Cato and Antony, was of course very vast. Plutarch both read widely—including some Latin[2]—and had access to sources of living tradition, both in his Greek milieu and at Rome. He had more than enough to fill his mould generously. He did however keep to the same type of mould. Although these Lives tend to be longer than most others, they are constructed on the principles we have seen. There will be a consistent, perhaps naïve, interpretation of character and a clear view of the great climaxes and turning-points (*metabolai*) of the career. Narrative history merely provides the background. But the morality is played on a larger stage. Roman

[1] *Galba* I.   [2] cf. above, p. 54.

history is world history. What Plutarch says in *The Fortune of the Romans* gives the key to his treatment of Roman affairs:

The mighty *daimōn*[3] of Rome did not blow fair for a day nor flourish for a space like that of Macedon, nor on dry land only like that of Sparta, nor at sea only like that of Athens. It was not roused late like the *daimōn* of Persia, nor cease early like the *daimōn* of Colophon.[4] From the first beginnings it grew and flourished with the city; it stayed constant on sea and land, in war and peace, against barbarians and against Greeks. (324B)

The characters and events have a cosmic stature. Plutarch soaks up the colour of his sources, often sombre and lurid. The dramatic and rhetorical tradition of Greek historiography had been nurtured on the vast events of Alexander's empire and the vicissitudes of his successor kings. Rome was an even grander subject. Thus there are many sudden changes of fortune in Plutarch, especially in the 'Hellenistic' Lives, *Demetrius* and *Pyrrhus*; but none is more spectacular than the scene with Marius after the victory of Aquae Sextiae (*Marius* 22–3):

He piled the remainder of the spoil on a huge pyre and carried out a magnificent sacrifice. As the troops stood by under arms, wearing garlands, Marius himself in his purple-edged toga took a burning torch in both hands, raised it to the sky, and was on the point of setting it to the pyre, when some friends were seen riding in haste towards him. Silence fell; everyone waited. The newcomers leaped from their horses and embraced Marius. They were the bearers of the good news that he had been elected consul for the fifth time . . . Yet Fortune, or Nemesis, or Cosmic Necessity, that never allows success to enjoy undiluted pleasure, but diversifies the life of man with mingled good and evil, brought Marius within a few days the news of his colleague Catulus.

Catulus had been defeated in a monstrous battle of giants, in which the Gauls had vanquished the elements, dammed rivers and overrun the countryside like a flood.

[3] Here 'guardian spirit', but not easily differentiated from Fortune (*tuchē*).

[4] Colophon, proverbial for its pride and splendour, fell, with the other Ionian cities first under Lydia and then under Persia. It is a stock example in early poets for 'pride before a fall': e.g. Theognis 1103–4; and cf. Athenaeus 12.526C.

Marius, like his pair Pyrrhus, is a plaything of fortune. But, unlike the Greek, he is an elemental, barbaric force, that finally comes crashing down into disgrace and savagery. Most Romans, for Plutarch, had a potentiality for barbarism; it is part of his picture of the Greco-Roman symbiosis that Greek *paideia* is the prime means of neutralising this risk. The closing scenes of Marius' life combine drama of situation with psychological analysis. Among Plutarch's sources was the general history of 146–96 B.C. written by the philosopher Posidonius, himself a witness of Marius' old age, and a vivid stylist. The overall picture and the selection and the grouping of detail seem, however, to be Plutarch's own; and both language and thought show traces of the influence of Plato—always an important factor in such picturesque and heightened writing.

At this juncture, the senate met and sent envoys to Cinna and Marius, asking them to enter Rome and spare the people. Cinna was consul, and so it was he who gave audience to the envoys from his official chair, while Marius stood at one side, saying nothing, but showing by his grim face and repellent look that he was going to fill the city with bloodshed once again. When they broke up the meeting, and moved in, Cinna entered with his guards. Marius paused at the gate. He was an exile, he declared with angry sarcasm, forbidden to enter his native city. If his presence was needed, there must be another vote to rescind the vote of banishment. After all, he was a law-abiding man, and Rome was a free country! . . . But before three or four tribes had voted, he threw aside the pretence and the legalistic talk of exile, and entered the city with a picked bodyguard of the slaves who had joined his forces, whom he called Bardyaei.[5] These men murdered many at a word from Marius, many indeed at a mere nod . . . The corpses were thrown headless into the streets and trampled. Yet no one felt pity— only horror and trembling at the sight . . . But the wind, as it were, was changing. News came from every quarter that Sulla had brought the war against Mithridates to a conclusion, recovered the provinces, and started on his way home with a large force . . . Marius was elected consul for the seventh time . . . Exhausted by hardship, swamped and wearied with anxiety, he could not bring his mind to face the monstrous

[5] After a savage tribe in Illyria.

prospect of renewed war and fresh conflicts of which his experience of fatigue and danger now made him terrified. This would be no trial of strength with an Octavius or a Merula with their hotch-potch rabble and factious mob. Sulla was coming—Sulla, who had once before driven him out and had now forced Mithridates back to the Black Sea. These thoughts brought him to a breakdown; his long wanderings and exile, the dangers of his flight over land and sea were constantly before his eyes. He fell into a state of utter helplessness, visited by nightly panics and disturbing dreams, in which he was always imagining someone saying

'Dread is the lair though the lion is gone.'[6]

Yet most of all he dreaded his insomnia, and to keep it at bay plunged into bouts of drinking at all hours on a scale quite unsuitable to a man of his years, trying to make sleep a refuge from his anxieties.[7] Ultimately, when a courier arrived from the coast, fresh fears would assail him, partly out of anxiety for the future, partly because the burden of the present had become intolerable. It did not take much to tip the scale. He succumbed to pleurisy, as we are told by the philosopher Posidonius who says that he visited Marius during his illness and discussed his diplomatic business with him ... Some say that his ambition was manifested in his illness, and broke out in an extraordinary delusion: he imagined he was commanding an army in the Mithridatic war, and made all sorts of gestures and movements of his body, shouting and screaming loud and often, just as he used to do in the heat of battle. So fierce and inconsolable was the passion for that particular field of action that his jealousy and love of power had planted in him! (43–5)

Heightened and emotional narrative is a feature of many of these Lives. Scenery and weather contribute to effects which could intelligibly be called not only 'sublime' but 'baroque'.[8] *Crassus* is particularly rich in this kind of thing. Crassus goes into hiding in a cave (4); the description is a quite elaborate piece of landscape, with echoes of the scenarios of Plato's *Phaedrus* and *Laws*, and going a good way beyond the need to make it clear that

[6] An unknown hexameter line: epic or an oracle?
[7] cf. Plutarch's account of the neurosis of the superstitious, above p. 99.
[8] See the suggestive remarks of P. Scazzoso, *Actes du VIIIe Congrès . . . Budé*, 569 ff.

it was a secure and well-lit retreat with its own water-supply. We observe too the evocative description of a desert-crossing (22) and the horrific thunderstorm at the passage of the Euphrates (19), where the camp-site is twice struck by lightning and a richly-caparisoned horse vanishes under the angry surges of the river. Most astonishing of all is the gusto with which Plutarch takes up the scene of the Parthian mock triumph (32):

C. Paccianus, the captive who most resembled Crassus, put on a woman's royal dress and was instructed to answer to the name of Crassus and the title Imperator. He was seated on a led horse, with trumpeters and lictors riding before him on camels. From the fasces hung leather bags and on the axes were fresh Roman severed heads. Behind followed girl-musicians from Seleucia, chanting ridiculous insults against Crassus' effeminacy and cowardice . . . Surenas also assembled the Council of Seleucia, and produced before it some indecent books—Aristides' *Milesian Tales*.[9] There was no deception in this. They had indeed been found in Rustius' baggage, and afforded Surenas many humorous insults at the Romans' expense. The citizens of Seleucia, however, came to appreciate the wisdom of Aesop,[10] as they observed Surenas with his wallet of Milesian indecencies in front, but dragging behind him a Parthian Sybaris, all those wagon-loads of concubines—a monster the very opposite of the vipers and serpents we read of, for while spearmen and archers and cavalry made the forepart of the creature fearsome and awe-inspiring, it tailed off behind into dances and tambourines, music and nightly orgies with the ladies . . .

This leads up to the most famous scene of all: the actor Jason dancing and singing in the part of Agaue in the *Bacchae*—using Crassus' head for Pentheus':

Such was the epilogue that ended the tragedy of Crassus' command. (33.7)

But in no Life is this heightening of emotional tone more

[9] A collection of erotic short stories, translated into Latin, and evidently popular with the Romans.

[10] In the fable in which every man is said to carry two wallets, one in front, containing other people's ills, and one behind, containing his own: Phaedrus 4.10, Babrius 66.

conspicuous than in *Antony*. This, with its pair *Demetrius*, is explicitly a 'deterrent' Life:

It is perhaps not a bad thing to include in our models of lives (*paradeigmata biōn*—a revealing description of the genre) a pair (*suzugia*) or two of those who have used themselves imprudently and become notable for viciousness in power and high affairs. (*Demetrius* 1)

Moreover, its main point concerns the corruptions of *erōs* and the effects of *kolakeia* (flattery). But, unlike Alcibiades, the hero is not the *kolax*: he is the victim of the *kolakeia* of Cleopatra. Naïve as this seems, it is the hub of Plutarch's interpretation. The brilliance of the writing, the inspired choice of material, the gusto and magnificence, all make us forget it; but basically *Antony* is a simple cautionary tale. It could properly be subtitled *The World Ill Lost*.

Plutarch was fortunate in many of his sources. Q. Dellius, the vivid but businesslike historian of the Parthian war, was a key figure in the story: an eye-witness of many of the events, a supporter of Antony who finally went over to Octavian (59), and the supposed author of *epistulae lascivae* to Cleopatra—the sort of book that may lie behind the details of *Antony* 25. Besides this, there were eye-witness accounts of the final drama in Alexandria; in this connection, Plutarch mentions Cleopatra's doctor Olympus (82), and he may well be the authority for much more than the detail for which he is quoted. And finally, there were certain personal recollections passed on by Plutarch's grandfather (28).

Most of his sources, naturally enough, were hostile. The histories had been written, for the most part, in the full light of the Augustan victory. Of earlier sources, Cicero's *Philippics* were a classic, the greatest Latin invective; Plutarch draws on them (9), but also criticises (6.1): Antony was *not* the Helen of the Civil War. But the generally unfavourable portrait that results from the political bias of the sources and the moral prejudices of the author does not exclude the recognition of Antony's good qualities: his courage, generosity and humanity. It is this of course that makes Plutarch's Antony a potential tragic hero, not an unsympathetic adventurer.

Now these virtues, like the faults, were to some extent family characteristics. Plutarch is interested in heredity,[11] and here he has an example to hand. He therefore opens the Life with an anecdote of the open-handed generosity of Antony's father, and closes it with a reminder of the fifth generation of his posterity, the matricidal lunatic Nero, who 'came near to overthrowing the empire' in Plutarch's own lifetime.

The corruption of Antony begins early, with the pernicious companionship first of Curio and then of Clodius. But the principal influences on him at all times were women. His first wife, Fulvia, dominant and powerful, moulds him and prepares him for his subsequent subjection to Cleopatra (10.3). Octavia, the second wife, is seen throughout as a foil to Cleopatra, the good fairy hopefully but unsuccessfully countering the bad.

The turning-point in Antony's career is therefore the sequence of events that led to his meeting with Cleopatra in 41 B.C. (24):

Leaving L. Censorinus in charge of Greece, he crossed to Asia and laid his hands on the treasures to be found there. Kings waited at his door, royal ladies vied in gifts and beauty and languished for him. While Octavian was wearing himself out with wars and conflicts in Rome, Antony had abundant leisure and peace. He reverted emotionally to his wonted ways. Lute-players like Anaxenor, flautists like Xuthus, a dancer named Metrodorus, a whole company of Asian entertainments, flooded into and controlled his court, far surpassing in impudence and rude humour the evil geniuses he brought from Italy. Everything was concentrated on these excesses; it was an intolerable situation. The whole of Asia, like the city in Sophocles, was

full of offerings of incense,
full too of hymns and groans of grief.[12]

When he entered Ephesus, men in the guise of Pans and Satyrs and women dressed as Bacchanals led the way. The town was full of ivy and thyrsuses, harps and pipes and flutes. He was hailed as Dionysus, 'the kindly, the giver of joy'. And that indeed was his character towards some, while towards others he was Dionysus the Savage, the Devourer.

---

[11] *God's Slowness to Punish*, 561C–563B.
[12] *Oedipus Tyrannus* 4.

For he would take property from the nobility to bestow it on criminals and flatterers. Some people in fact succeeded in assuming the death of persons who were still alive and in claiming their estates. And Antony is said to have presented the house of a Magnesian citizen to a chef who had earned his commendation for a single good dinner. Ultimately, when he was imposing an additional tribute on the cities, Hybreas ventured to speak out for Asia. The style was vulgar—agreeable indeed to Antony's taste.[13] 'If you can take tribute twice a year,' said the orator, 'you can give us two summers and two autumns.' The conclusion was both paradoxical and relevant to the facts: Asia had given two hundred thousand talents. 'If you never received it, ask for it from those who did. If you received it but have not got it, we are ruined.' This made a strong impression on Antony, who was in fact ignorant of much of what was going on, not because he was lazy, but because his naïveté led him to place confidence in those around him.

For there was indeed a naïveté in his character. He was slow to notice; but when he discovered his mistakes, violent self-recrimination followed, in which he admitted his errors to those who had suffered from them. There was a grandeur about both his rewards and his punishments, though it was in granting favours rather than in inflicting punishment that he was held to go beyond the mean. One could exchange jokes and even insults with him; he was as happy to be laughed at as to laugh. This indeed damaged his affairs on many occasions. Unable to believe that people who had joked with him so frankly were flattering him with serious intent, he was easily captivated by their praise. He did not realize that some people used frankness as a kind of astringent sauce for flattery to take away the cloying effect. The object, in fact, of their bold chatter over their cups was to ensure that the submissive agreement on points of policy which was to follow should be taken, not as a token of complaisance, but as the effect of a rational submission to superior wisdom.

This description, with its echoes of the themes of *Friends and Flatterers*,[14] is evidently largely Plutarch's construction, even if a certain amount of it comes from Hybreas' speech. It leads directly to the crowning instance of Antony's susceptibility to *kolakeia* (25):

[13] Hybreas of Mylasa, an orator in the Asianic style, is known also from the elder Seneca, who excerpts a few passages. Octavian ridiculed Antony's 'mad' style (Suet. *Aug.* 86).
[14] cf. above, pp. 94 ff.

Such was the Antony on whom descended the ultimate disaster of love for Cleopatra. This love roused and stirred into frenzy many emotions hitherto concealed and dormant in him, while it nullified and obliterated what good or saving qualities still resisted. This is how he was captured: At the outset of his Parthian campaign he sent to her, ordering her to meet him in Cilicia to answer charges of having made gifts and contributions to Cassius for war purposes. When Dellius, who was the messenger, saw Cleopatra's appearance, and observed her skill and subtlety in conversation, he immediately perceived that Antony would not so much as contemplate harming a woman like this; on the contrary, she would have great influence with him. Dellius therefore addressed himself to courting the queen, and urging her to come to Cilicia, 'decking herself out fair', as Homer says[15] and not to be afraid of Antony, who was the most charming and kind of generals. Cleopatra consented. The earlier associations which her beauty had enabled her to form with Caesar and with Pompey's son Gnaeus, led her to think that it would be easy to reduce Antony to submission. When they had known her, she had been but a girl, inexperienced in the ways of the world. Now she was at the time of life when women combine their most dazzling beauty with the height of their mental powers.[16] She got ready her gifts, her money, her finery, on a scale appropriate to a great estate and a wealthy kingdom; but it was in her own person and its charms and glamour that she placed the greatest confidence.

Antony and his friends had sent her many invitations; but she merely laughed at him and treated him with disdain. She sailed up the Cydnus in a barge with a gilded stern. The sails were purple, the rowers plied oars of silver to the music of flute and pipe and lyre. The queen lay under a gold-spangled awning, dressed as Aphrodite, while boys like the Cupids in paintings stood beside her and fanned her. The most beautiful of her maids, dressed as Nereids and Graces, were grouped round the tiller and the tackling. Wonderful perfume from burning incense wafted over the riverside. On both banks, all the way up from the estuary, the local people kept pace with her progress, or came flocking from the city to see her. The *agora* [of Tarsus] gradually emptied, until Antony was left alone in his official chair. The word went round that Aphrodite was paying a festal visit to Dionysus for the good of Asia . . .

[15] Of Hera preparing herself for Zeus: *Iliad* 14.162.
[16] She was 28. The affair with Caesar was about eight years earlier.

'The barge she sat on, like a burnish'd throne, burned on the water' . . . Shakespeare made this scene his own; he added conceits, play of language, poetical conciseness. But there is hardly anything in his version that is not in Plutarch, at least in the English Plutarch that North made out of Amyot's French.[17] This is unusual closeness to a 'source'; perhaps Shakespeare saw not only that it is a splendid piece and a memorable tableau, but also that it is the keystone of Plutarch's structure.

The dénouement is of course long delayed: by the intervention of Octavia (31), and by the Parthian war (33–50). When the military narrative is ended, the strings of the plot are again drawn together. Antony waits for Cleopatra in Lebanon; he is nerve-racked and dependent now on drink (51). The rivalry between Octavia and Cleopatra moves to a head (53–4), and with it war between Antony and Octavian becomes inevitable. The causes of the war are seen personally rather than politically. The moral is crudely drawn. Immediately after enumerating the contending forces, the kingdoms and provinces which Antony controlled, from the Euphrates to Illyria, from Cyrene to Ethiopia, Plutarch goes on (62.1):

But so much was he the mere appendage of the lady that, despite his superiority on land, he wanted the main issue to lie with the fleet, for Cleopatra's sake. And yet he could see that, because of the shortage of crews, the captains were conscripting from long-suffering Greece travellers, donkey-drivers, harvest-workers and students (*ephēboi*)— and even so the ships were not fully manned!

Plutarch here probably draws on family or local tradition;[18] he piquantly deduces the sufferings of his people from Antony's infatuation with 'the lady'. The donkey-drivers and harvesters stand in ironic contrast to the princes and kings of the army-list that precedes.

Much mystery surrounds the campaign of Actium; neither Plutarch nor any other source gives a clear account. Plutarch

[17] Text, with comment, in G. Bullough, *Narrative and Dramatic Sources of Shakespeare*, vol. v, 1964, 271 ff. See below, Chapter 9.
[18] cf. *Antony* 58; above, p. 1.

concentrates steadily on the personal aspect. For the sequel, the days of abandonment and death, he evidently had good first-hand evidence; perhaps not only Olympus, but the rhetor Aristocrates and the Roman Lucilius, Antony's companions (9.1), left written record.

Leaving his misanthropic retreat at Pharos (69–70), Antony plunges again into court life (71), and he and Cleopatra dine with their friends in the club of 'partners in death' (71). The war is quiescent, until, in the spring of 30 B.C., Octavian approaches Alexandria. There is an unexpected success, soon shattered by treachery:

Caesar had taken up position near the race-course; Antony sallied out and fought a brilliant battle, routing Caesar's cavalry and chasing them back to camp. He returned to the palace in high spirits at this success, kissed Cleopatra even before taking off his armour, and presented to her the man who had fought with greatest distinction. Cleopatra gave the soldier a golden breastplate and helmet as a reward. He took them —and deserted to Caesar that night.

Next, Antony sent Caesar a new challenge to single combat, to which Caesar replied that Antony had many roads of death open to him. Antony himself felt that none was better than battle; and he resolved to make an attempt by land and by sea simultaneously ... About midnight that night, when the city lay under an oppressive calm, in anxious expectation of what was to come, there was a sudden sound of music (it is said) from all kinds of instruments, together with the shouting of a crowd, with howling and leaping like that of satyrs, as though some Bacchic troop was noisily making off. The commotion passed through almost the whole of the city centre as far as the gate facing the enemy, where the noise was loudest and then disappeared. The common interpretation of this was that the god [Dionysus] to whom Antony had most assimilated and linked himself was now abandoning him.

At daybreak, he stationed the infantry on the hills in front of the city, and watched his ships put out and move towards the enemy. He waited quietly, hoping to see them in action. But when they got near, they saluted Caesar's fleet with their oars. The salute was returned. Antony's men changed sides, and the united fleet advanced towards the city ready for action. (74.4–76.2)

Antony, defeated on land as well, accuses Cleopatra. She flees to the tomb and sends word that she is dead. He believes the message, and says to himself:

'Antony, why are you still waiting? Fortune has taken the one remaining excuse for clinging to life.' He went into his room, and unfastened and put away his breastplate. 'O Cleopatra,' he said; 'I am not grieved that you are taken from me. I shall soon come to you. But it does grieve me that a general like myself should be found inferior in courage to a woman.' He had a reliable servant named Eros, whom he had long ago engaged to kill him if he ever needed it. Now he asked for the fulfilment of the promise. Eros drew his sword and raised it as though to strike. But then he turned away and killed himself, falling at Antony's feet. 'Well done, Eros,' said he; 'you could not do it yourself, but you teach me to do what I must.' He drove the sword into his stomach and fell back on the bed. It was not a wound to bring an easy death. When he lay down, the flow of blood stopped. He came to, and begged the people around to give him the final blow. But they ran out of the room, while he shouted and writhed, until Diomedes the secretary came from Cleopatra, with orders to take him to the tomb. He thus realized that Cleopatra was alive, and anxiously asked the attendants to lift him up. He was carried in their arms to the door of the building. Cleopatra did not open the door but appeared at a window and let down ropes and cords. They fastened Antony to these, and Cleopatra herself and the two women she had taken with her into the tomb pulled him up. Eye-witnesses tell us there never was a more pitiful sight. He was covered in blood and dying painfully, stretching out his arms towards her as he dangled in the air. Nor was it easy work for women; Cleopatra, her hands clinging to the rope, her face strained, could scarcely pull the rope in. The people down below were shouting encouragement and sharing the agony. When she had thus taken him in and laid him down, she tore her clothes over him; beating and rending her breast with her hands, plastering the blood over her face, she called him 'lord' and 'husband' and 'general'. Indeed she nearly forgot her own troubles in her pity for his. But Antony put a stop to her lamentation and asked for a drink of wine. Perhaps he was thirsty; perhaps he thought it would make a quicker release. When he had drunk it, he gave her his advice: to see to the security of her own affairs if she could do so honourably, and to trust Proculeius especially among Caesar's friends; and not to grieve for him at this last change, but to reckon him happy for all the blessings he had enjoyed; he had been a famous man, and a man of great power; and now he had been defeated without disgrace by a fellow Roman. (76.5–77)

This is a magnificent scene. Plutarch's stately periods (which I have mercilessly, but necessarily, broken up) prove (like Livy's) a good vehicle for the accumulation and organisation of just the detail that makes a vivid and unforgettable picture. But the light is concentrated almost exclusively on the two main characters; the rest of the crowded scene is visible only vaguely, an anxious but anonymous and inactive circle of synagonistic 'persons present'. This is characteristic of ancient narrative; one thinks not only of tragic choruses but of the Athenians watching the desperate sea-battle at Syracuse in the last phases of the Sicilian disaster.[19] It is a limitation in realism, but one that Plutarch shares with the entire tradition of ancient literature.[20]

I add one point. Let us set beside this narrative the moralising comment on Antony's death that Plutarch makes in the *Comparison with Demetrius*:

As for their deaths, neither is to be praised, though Demetrius deserves more blame, because he allowed himself to be taken prisoner, and was pleased to win three years extra in captivity; he was tamed, like an animal, by wine and through his belly. Antony, on the other hand, took himself off in a cowardly, pitiful and dishonourable fashion; but at least he did not let his enemy obtain possession of his person. (6.3–4)

It is one of the paradoxes of Plutarch that he can do these two things: the moving narrative, with its suspense and pathos, its apt and concise detail; and also the crude and prudish moral. This is that *naïveté de l'âme* which has often baffled or amused adult sophistication. There is something childlike in the combination of vivid imagination, splendid words, and banal censoriousness. We have to come to terms with this, perhaps even to turn a blind eye, if we are to respond rightly.

[19] Thucydides 7.71.
[20] Some related points are made by E. Auerbach, *Mimesis*, chs. 1–3.

CHAPTER NINE

From Plutarch to Shakespeare

THE only serious attempt at a complete survey of Plutarch's influence is that of Rudolf Hirzel.[1] This is now sixty years old, and, though it is something of a masterpiece, it is out of date and incomplete. I shall make no attempt here to replace it. What follows is the merest outline of a vast subject; in it I have concentrated mainly on the judgments passed on Plutarch and the translations of his works. These are the outward and visible signs of fame. An author's 'influence' of course is not to be measured like this. It is always something elusive and indefinable, and particularly so with Plutarch, because of the nature of what he did. Madame Roland observed: 'Plutarque m'avait disposée pour devenir républicaine'—and he was indeed a widely admired and inspiring author in the context of French republicanism. But Hirzel's comment[2] is pertinent, and of wider application: it was antiquity, not Plutarch, that had this effect on her, but antiquity seen 'in and through Plutarch, with his eyes'. It is this that makes the specifically Plutarchan contribution to the intellectual stock of any generation so difficult to isolate.

Plutarch died a famous man. His reputation in the society in which he had lived was assured by his learning and the moral tone of his writings. His personal distinction and the success of his family no doubt helped to keep it alive. There are plenty of second-century witnesses. Aulus Gellius draws both on the *Lives* and on

---

[1] *Plutarch*, 74–206. The book is in the series *Das Erbe der Alten*, and accordingly Hirzel devotes two-thirds of it to Plutarch's *Nachwirken*.
[2] op. cit., p. 161.

other works; to one of his characters, the philosopher Taurus, 'our Plutarch' is 'a man most learned and most wise'.[3] In the reign of Marcus Aurelius, a certain Amyntianus wrote 'parallels' in imitation of Plutarch's: Dionysius and Domitian, Philip and Augustus.[4] Polyaenus' *Strategems* (A.D. 162) appropriates a good deal of *Brave Deeds of Women*.[5] But the most striking proof of fame in this period is the attribution to Plutarch of works like *Fate* and *Doctrines of the Philosophers* which have come down to us in the corpus of his writings. It is clear that he became a classic: a rare fate for an imperial writer, shared only by his contemporary Dion and the later sophist Aristides—and all the more remarkable because Plutarch's vocabulary was not acceptable to the stricter Atticisers.[6] When sophists criticise him, they do so, as they might Plato, as a representative philosopher with an acknowledged place in the literary pantheon. This is how he comes to appear by name in the curious letter of Philostratus to Julia Domna:

O empress, persuade Plutarch, whose audacity goes beyond Hellenic standards, not to be angry with the sophists . . .[7]

Plutarch continued to be read throughout the later empire, and especially in the schools of Athens. In the middle of the fourth century, when the sophist Himerius presented his son Rufinus to the Areopagus[8] he stressed the boy's maternal ancestry:

This is the descendant of Plutarch, through whom you educate all men.

'You' means 'you Athenians'. Athens is the school of the world, Plutarch her favourite text-book.

Both pagan and Christian writings of the later empire do in fact show many traces of him. This is true not only of Porphyry and Julian and the Neoplatonist commentators, but of Clement and

---

[3] *Attic Nights* 1.26: Plutarch is having a slave whipped, and the slave ventures to lecture him on the control of anger; Plutarch replies that he is not angry, but is quite prepared to continue the discussion while the whipping proceeds.

[4] Photius, cod. 131.

[5] P. A. Stadter, *Plutarch's Historical Methods*, 1965.

[6] e.g. *dusōpia* (cf. above, p. 112) was unacceptable to the grammarian Phrynichus.

[7] Epistle 63; C. P. Jones, *Plutarch and Rome*, 131. Translation uncertain: perhaps 'the most audacious member of the Hellenic race . . .'

[8] Oration 7.4; cf. 8.21.

Eusebius and, in a special degree, the Cappadocian fathers, Basil and the two Gregorys. There was much in his morals and theology that seemed to foreshadow the Christianity he never knew. A work like *The Decline of Oracles* gave plenty of opportunities for Christian comment. It was held, for instance, to prove the flight of the demons at the coming of the Saviour, for the oracles that had fallen silent were operated by *daimones*:

It is Plutarch who witnesses to this explicitly, Plutarch the Chaeronean, no Hebrew but a Greek in race and speech, enslaved to the opinions of the Greeks, and deeply versed in the errors concerning oracles; Delphi, Lebadea and Oropus are not far from Chaeronea.[9]

More specifically, the famous story of the death of Pan suggested a bold interpretation. Plutarch (419B) had told how an Egyptian pilot named Thamous had received instructions from a mysterious voice, heard off the island of Paxi, to call out, when they reached a certain place, 'Great Pan is dead...' He obeyed; a mighty groan was heard. For Plutarch, this illustrated the death of a *daimōn*; they were long-lived but not immortal. It was a circumstantial story, dated under Tiberius. The Christian interpretation in Eusebius[10] depends on the date: the *daimones* are the demons whom Christ chased out of the world. This is on the level of Christian views of Virgil's Fourth Eclogue, which was taken as a Messianic prophecy in the fourth century, and springs from the same concern to weld pagan classics into witnesses for the gospel. There is a footnote to this story. A millennium later, Rabelais invented—or so it seems—a variant allegorisation: Pan is Christ himself, because *pan* in Greek means 'all', and Christ is our all.[11]

It is clear that Plutarch remained standard reading throughout the late empire, down to the sixth or seventh century. His influence is more apparent among philosophers and Christian preachers than in orators and sophists: Libanius uses him little if at all, Julian a great deal. His popularity is evidenced also by his

[9] Theodoret, *Graecarum Affectionum Curatio* 10.5.
[10] *Praeparatio Evangelica* 5.17.
[11] *Pantagruel* 4.28; R. Flacelière, ed. of *The Decline of Oracles*, 79–87.

use in anthologies: Sopater of Apamea excerpted him largely;[12] Stobaeus too has a generous selection of the *Moralia*. Eunapius, who wrote lives of philosophers in the fifth century, regarded Plutarch as their greatest literary luminary, the charmer and musician of philosophy.[13] Syriac translations of *Control of Anger* and *How to Profit from Your Enemies* date apparently from the sixth century. The poet-historian Agathias (c. 536–82) thus stood in a continuous tradition of admiration for Plutarch when he wrote the epigram for a statue which Dryden translated:

> Chaeronean Plutarch, to thy deathless praise
> Doth martial Rome this grateful statue raise,
> Because both Greece and she thy fame have shared
> (Their heroes written and their lives compared).
> But thou thyself couldst never write thy own;
> Their lives have parallels, but thine has none.[14]

The transmission of Plutarch's text shows clearly that in a somewhat later period too, from the ninth century onwards, he was a much sought-after author. This is the age in which the collections of the Lives, as we have them, were formed, and also considerable collections of the miscellaneous works. The Lives were used both as historical models and as sources, for example by Zonaras in the twelfth century. Tzetzes in the depth of poverty chose to keep no book but a Plutarch[15]—anticipating, apparently, the later Greek humanist Theodorus Gazes, who is supposed to have told his friends that, if all books had to be lost save one, he would choose Plutarch to be saved.[16] And John Mauropus in the eleventh century prays in a poem that Christ, if He will save any pagan from wrath, may exempt Plato and Plutarch, the two who were by nature nearest to the law 'in doctrine and in character'.

[12] Photius, cod. 161.   [13] p. 346 Wright.
[14] *Anthologia Palatina* 16.331.
[15] If the story is true: K. Krumbacher, *Geschichte der Byzantinischen Literatur*, 235.
[16] This anecdote was popularised by Xylander; it is neatly parodied by Molière, *Les Femmes savantes* 2.7, where Chrysale will have all his books burned as useless 'hors un gros Plutarque, pour mettre mes rabats'.

But the most important figure is a later one, the Byzantine monk Maximus Planudes (*c.* 1255—*c.* 1305). A scholar in many fields, he resolved also to have Plutarch's works copied: 'I love the man so very much.' The operation had three stages. First, a collection of sixty-nine of the miscellaneous works was assembled from various manuscripts—some of which are themselves extant —to form the contents of a splendid codex now in Milan (Ambrosianus 859). This was finished before 1296. Secondly, Planudes planned a text of all that survived, both *Lives* and *Moralia*; it was finished in July 1296 and is the extant 'codex Parisinus 1671'. Planudes' services were not over; some time after 1302 he discovered two further manuscripts, one of *Table Talk*, the other containing eight important but apparently little-known books—including *A Book of Love*, *The Face in the Moon*, *Socrates' Sign*, and *Herodotus' Malice*. These were copied into a further comprehensive Plutarch, probably also written in Planudes' lifetime (codex Parisinus 1672). Without this discovery, much that most interests modern readers would have perished, for these few books extend our idea of his range very notably.

The story of Plutarch's fortunes in the West begins effectively two generations or so after Planudes. He had indeed been used by Macrobius, a writer much read in the Latin Middle Ages. And the name had been kept alive by the forged *Instructions to Trajan*, preserved by John of Salisbury, and most probably of Byzantine origin. But it was a set of epitomised Lives, in contemporary Greek, in Aragonese, and finally in Tuscan, that seems to have begun the vogue for Plutarch towards the end of the fourteenth century. These versions naturally had only local circulation; translation into Latin was the essential step to wider recognition, and this was for the most part a fifteenth-century achievement. Some isolated efforts were earlier: *Control of Anger* was translated by the monk Simon Attumanus[17] in papal Avignon around 1373. With the spread of Greek manuscripts in Italy in the fifteenth

[17] On his part in disseminating knowledge of Greek texts, see G. Zuntz, *Inquiry into the Transmission of the Plays of Euripides*, 284.

century, the *Lives* became a particularly popular work. Latin
versions (and epitomes)[18] rapidly accumulated in manuscript. A
complete Latin *Lives*, by various hands, was printed at Rome in
1470. These humanist *Lives* are pleasant reading, but sit loose to
the Greek and often abridge radically. The collection was supple-
mented by various extraneous items, including humanist imitations (D. Acciaiuoli's *Hannibal* and *Scipio*), which came to form
a part of many Latin and vernacular Plutarchs.

Early translations of the *Moralia* are comparatively few. But
Guarino's *Education of Children* dates from 1410, Coluccio
Salutati's *Progress in Virtue* and *Control of Anger* are even earlier
(before 1406), and if the anonymous Latin *Fortune of Alexander* is
by Jacopo Angeli de Scarperia, who died in 1411, it belongs to the
same period. A hundred years later, by contrast, translation of the
Moralia was a task which attracted the most distinguished minds.
Erasmus had assisted in the preparation of the Greek *editio
princeps*, the Aldine of 1509. It started a lifelong interest in
Plutarch. Not only did Erasmus translate a number of works, he
adapted and imitated constantly, especially in the *Adagia*. His
version of *Friends and Flatterers* was dedicated to Henry VIII in
1513, and a whole group of treatises to Wolsey the following
year. In 1525, *Control of Anger* and *Curiosity* were sent to Alexius
Turzo, treasurer of Hungary. The preface[19] contains an unusually
good account of Plutarch's style and the problems it presented:

I have found indeed very considerable difficulty in the subtlety of
Plutarch's language, the recondite ideas drawn from the inmost stores
of all authors and all disciplines, joined together in such a way that one
might regard it not as a style (*oratio*) but as a cento[20] or, to put it better,
a mosaic work (*musaicum opus*),[21] constructed of the most exquisite

[18] G. Resta, *Le epitomi di Plutarco nel quattrocento*, Padova 1962, with his
references. The epitomes were popular, and were still being printed in English
in the eighteenth century.

[19] P. S. Allen, *Opus Epistularum Erasmi*, no. 1572 (vi, 70 ff.).

[20] Erasmus uses the Latin *cento*—literally a patchwork blanket or the like—in
the sense it also bears in English, i.e. a composition made up of excerpts and
quotations.

[21] i.e. something like the patterns of shells set on walls of grottoes: cf. *Epist.*
756.17 Allen.

inlaid pieces (*emblēmata*). This was very easy for Plutarch, who had his head full of every kind of literary furniture, but it is very difficult for his translator to observe what he has culled from where, especially as most of the authors from whose fields he garnered the flowers with which he made these garlands are no longer extant. Apart from this difficulty, he possesses a certain conciseness and abruptness, suddenly shifting the reader's mind to a different area, so that he requires not only a reader of all-round learning but one who is also attentive and watchful.

The list of the Latin translators is indeed impressive.[22] It includes Politian and Melanchthon; Willibald Pirckheimer, Dürer's friend; in England, Sir John Cheke and the diplomat Richard Pace. By the middle of the century, practically the whole of the *Moralia* was in Latin: a variorum collection was printed at Paris in 1566.

It was however almost immediately superseded. Two German scholars, Xylander (i.e. Holzmann) and Cruserius, attempted, independently of each other, the whole work: Xylander's *Lives* appeared in 1561, his *Moralia* in 1570; Cruserius' *Lives* came out in 1564, his *Moralia* in 1573. Xylander's work was the more elegant, hence the more popular. These Latin translations are important. Not only did they reach an international public, which the vernacular versions could not, but most readers of Greek in all countries seem to have depended very much on Greco-Latin bilingual editions. It was both tempting and natural to read the Latin column, turning to the Greek only where there was some special need. Jeremy Taylor, a great reader and user of Plutarch as material for sermons, illustrates this neatly for a somewhat later period. It is noticeable that he commonly cites the embedded quotations in the original Greek, but Plutarch's own words in Xylander's Latin.

We saw that vernacular translation began early in Italy. In the early sixteenth century, while the labour of the Latinisers continued, Italian, French, Spanish, German and English versions were made from one another. They had a different audience from

[22] R. Aulotte, *Amyot et Plutarque*, 325 ff.

the Latin translations: court rather than college, women as well as men. Thus Sir Thomas Wyatt translated *Quyete of Mynde* (1528), and Sir Thomas Elyot, *The Education of Children* (1530). At the end of the century, Queen Elizabeth herself translated *Curiosity* (1598), quite in the spirit of the humanism in which she was brought up. Far the most influential version however was the French of Jacques Amyot (1513–93). It was a decisive event when this lifelong scholar and successful cleric turned from the Greek novelists to Plutarch's *Lives*. His complete version, dedicated to Henri II, appeared in 1559. The *Moralia* followed in 1572. Amyot worked directly from the Greek, though he naturally consulted the Latin versions, and also earlier French ones where these existed. His translation of the *Lives* indeed preceded Xylander's, and he made countless original contributions to the interpretation, and sometimes the reading, of the text. It has not always been easy for later editors to do him justice; and it is still not uncommon to find an emendation of modern date which turns out to be presupposed by Amyot's French.

His Preface is instructive. It is concerned largely with the usefulness of history, and of Plutarch in particular, to kings and princes. They are people who have to take great decisions, but often they have not been able in youth to devote themselves to 'the noble ancient tongues and the laborious disciplines that philosophy comprises'. Hence they need historians in their native language, to counterbalance the ill effects of flattery and lack of travel—for in this respect too princes have less opportunity than common men. They need not only history proper, which deals with deeds and events, but also lives, which are concerned with the nature, sayings and manners of men, their domestic life, their inner motives, their thoughts and counsels. In this department, Plutarch is supreme: a learned man, who occupied himself in public affairs and gave advice to the emperor Trajan, finally turning himself to writing the *Lives* that are 'a treasure of all rare and exquisite literature'.

Amyot took the stylistic duties of a translator seriously, and it is important to see how he conceived them. He makes two points which at first sight do not go too well together. On the one hand, the translator's 'office'

lies not only in faithfully rendering the sense of his author, but also in representing in some way and adumbrating his form of style and manner of speaking.

On the other hand:

I can give assurance that, however harsh or rude the language, my translation will be much easier to Frenchmen than the original Greek, even to those who are most exercised in the Greek language, because of a manner of writing proper to Plutarch which is rather acute, learned and compressed than clear, polished or easy.

It is therefore no betrayal of trust in Amyot's view, to add ease and facility. He did this partly by additions and interpretations, the innumerable *c'est-à-dire* of which his critics complained.[23] But more pervasively he did it by the structure of his prose, breaking the periodic form and freeing the detail from its antithetical or balancing function; this produces formal differences from Plutarch that result in a profoundly changed impression. It is arguable that Amyot is a greater writer than Plutarch. He is certainly a creator in a new literary language rather than a quasi-archaist in an old one. In any case, the Plutarch that he created, and that his enthusiastic admirer Montaigne[24] popularised, was something new and exciting.

England owes its Plutarch to two translators in Amyot's tradition. Thomas North, who was about twenty years Amyot's junior, went to France in 1574 in the entourage of his elder brother, Roger Lord North, who headed a special embassy to the French court. Amyot's versions would then be fresh in Paris. Thomas North set himself the task of translating them into English. The work appeared in 1579, later editions in 1595 and 1603. He did not consult the Greek, probably not even the Latin. In the sixteenth century no one would think this reprehensible; it was a normal

[23] Notably Bachet de Méziriac (1635) in a long essay on Amyot's errors (printed in *Menagiana*, 1715, II 425).
[24] The basic work is still P. Villey, *Amyot et Montaigne*, 1907.

procedure. Hence the Plutarch that Shakespeare read was basically Amyot's, but with a vigour and independence in the English, for North too had an enviable style.

The corpus of the *Moralia* had to wait a little longer. Philemon Holland (1552–1637), headmaster of the grammar school at Coventry, produced translations of a number of authors in the first decade of the new century; his *Moralia* dates from 1603. It is not a translation of Amyot, but Amyot's influence on it is immense.

Two passages from Ben Jonson neatly illustrate the familiarity of Plutarch in Jacobean England. In *The Devil is an Ass* (1616), one of the characters names his son Plutarchus, and explains why:

> That year, sir,
> That I begot him, I bought Plutarch's *Lives*,
> And fell so in love with the book, I called my son
> By his name, in hope he should be like him
> And write the lives of our great men.

The *Moralia* get a less favourable comment. In the opening scene of *The Silent Woman* (1609), the moral platitudes of Truewit elicit from Clerimont a reaction of disgust:

Foh! Thou hast read Plutarch's Morals now, or some such tedious fellow; and it shows so vilely with thee, 'fore God, 'twill spoil thy wit utterly.

The creative translation of Amyot and his English satellites is perhaps the most important event in the history of Plutarch's fortunes. However much they distorted him, the sixteenth-century translators made him a vernacular classic. Other versions, both English and French, followed and supplanted them; but it was they who made Plutarch the inheritance not only of scholars but of men and women of the world.

What they did is best seen in an example. Let us consider a chapter of *Antony* (29); I take it section by section, giving (*a*) a very bald version, retaining as far as possible the constructions; (*b*) Amyot; (*c*) North; (*d*) some notes on detail.

1. (*a*) But Cleopatra, dividing flattery not, as Plato says, into four, but into many parts, for ever bringing some new pleasure or gratification to bear upon him, both when he was engaged in serious business and when he was engaged in sport, led Antony like a child, never letting him go, night or day.

  (*b*) Mais *pour revenir* à Cléopâtre, Platon *écrit que l'art et la science* de flatter *se traite* en quatre manières; toutefois elle en *inventa beaucoup* plus de sortes: car fût ou en jeu, ou *en affaire de* conséquence, elle trouvait toujours quelque nouvelle volupté par laquelle elle *tenait sous sa main et maîtrisait* Antoine, ne l'abandonnant *jamais*, et *jamais* ne le perdant *de vue* ni de jour ni de nuit.

  (*c*) But *now again* to Cleopatra. Plato *wryteth that* there are foure kinds of flatterie: but Cleopatra divided it into many kinds. For she, were it in sport or *in matter of* earnest, still devised sundrie new delights to have Antonius *at commaundement*, never leaving him night nor day, nor once letting him go *out of her sight*.

(*d*) I have italicised the principal expansions and changes. It will be seen that North follows most of them, but not all; and in one place his 'divided' is closer to the Greek than Amyot's 'inventa'. The reference to Plato (*Gorgias* 464c) is a characteristic Plutarchan touch: the real fact improves upon the literary allusion. Amyot chooses a natural way of making the transition, but it does of course lose the 'grandeur' of the original. The word rendered 'led like a child' (*diepaidagōgei*) is common in Plutarch in a metaphorical sense, and the metaphor may be faded enough to justify omitting the notion of 'child'.

2. (*a*) She played dice with him and drank with him and hunted with him and watched him exercise in armour and wandered and roamed around with him in the dress of a maidservant as he went up to the doors and windows of townspeople at night and jeered at those in the house. For he too tried to dress himself up in that style. Hence he always returned having suffered mockery, and often blows.

  (*b*) Car elle jouait aux dés, elle buvait, elle chassait *ordinairement* avec lui, *elle était toujours présente* quand il prenait quelque exercice *de la personne*; quelquefois *qu'il se déguisait en valet* pour aller la nuit rôder par la ville, et *s'amuser* aux fenêtres et aux huis *des boutiques des petites gens mécaniques*, *à contester et railler* avec ceux qui étaient dedans, elle prenait l'accoutrement de quelque chambrière, et s'en allait *battre le pavé* et courir avec lui, dont il revenait toujours avec quelques moqueries, et bien souvent avec des coups *qu'on lui donnait*.

(c) For she would play at dyce with him, drinke with him, and hunt *commonly* with him, and also *be with him* when he went to any exercise *or activity of body*. And sometimes also, *when he would go up and down the city disguised like a slave* in the night, and would peere into poor men's windowes *and their shops*, and *scold and brawl* with them within the house; Cleopatra would also be seen in a chamber maides array, and amble up and downe the streets with him, so that oftentimes Antonius bare away *both mockes and blowes*.

(d) North takes up many of Amyot's expansions and changes: the addition of *ordinairement*; the substitution of 'being with him' for 'watching him' at exercise; the rendering of *'arms* exercise' by *de la personne*. More important, he adopts the transposition to an earlier stage of the statement that Antony was himself disguised as a slave on these nocturnal expeditions. This is very awkward, and slightly obscure, in Plutarch's Greek. Both translators define the social setting: Amyot with *boutiques* and *petites gens mécaniques*, North less picturesquely. North does however skimp here and there. He leaves out 'doors' and misses the antithesis *toujours/ bien souvent* in the last sentence. Here and there he omits a duplication: once—'exercise and activity'—he adds one.

3. (a) Most people looked on this with suspicion. The Alexandrians however enjoyed his buffoonery (*bōmolochia*) and joined in the fun, not without elegance and taste, liking it and saying that he used his tragic mask towards the Romans and his comic mask towards them.

(b) Et combien que cela *déplût et* fût suspect à la plupart, toutefois *communément* ceux d'Alexandrie étaient bien aises de cette joyeuseté, et la prenaient en bonne part, disant élégamment et ingénieusement qu'Antoine leur montrait un visage comique, *c'est-à-dire joyeux*, et aux Romains un tragique, *c'est-à-dire austère*.

(*c*) Now though most men misliked this maner, yet the Alexandrians were commonly glad of this jolity and liked it well, saying *verie gallantly and wisely*: that Antonius showed them a commicall face, *to wit, a merie countenance*, and the Romanes a tragicall face, *to say, a grimme look*.

(*d*) The main point one observes here is the *c'est-à-dire* expansion in the last sentence: Amyot and North explain the terms 'tragic' and 'comic', and mistranslate *prosōpon* as 'face' rather than 'mask'. *Bōmolochia* is a term for distinctively rude humour; *joyeuseté* and 'jolity' seem not quite to hit this off.

4. (*a*) To relate many of the jokes he played then would be much nonsense (*phluaros*).

   (*b*) Si serait trop grande simplesse *de vouloir ramasser et* réciter tous les ébattements *qu'ils firent* lors *en se jouant; mais j'en raconterai seulement un entre les autres.*

   (*c*) But to reckon up all the foolishe sportes *they* made, *revelling in this sorte*, it were too fond a parte of me, *and therefore I will only tell you one among the rest.*

(*d*) This extensive expansion is typical of the treatment of transitional passages (cf. section 1, above). It is one of the devices that tend to exaggerate the casualness of Plutarch, and make him seem a more leisurely story-teller than he is. Two small points: (*i*) *phluaros* is a harsher and more condemnatory word than *simplesse* or 'fond' seems to be; (*ii*) in Plutarch it is Antony who 'plays' these games, in the translators it is Antony *and Cleopatra*.

5. (*a*) But once, when, fishing and having no catch, he was annoyed because Cleopatra was present, he ordered the fishermen to swim down and secretly attach to the hook some fish which had been caught previously, and, pulling up two or three times, he did not escape the Egyptian lady's notice.

   (*b*) Il se mit quelquefois à pêcher à la ligne, et *voyant qu'il* ne pouvait rien prendre, en était fort dépit *et marri*, à cause que Cléopâtre était présente. Si commanda *secrètement* à quelques pêcheurs, *quand il aurait jeté sa ligne*, qu'ils allassent accrocher à son hameçon quelque poisson de ceux qu'ils auraient pêchés auparavant, et puis retira ainsi deux ou trois fois sa ligne avec prise. *Cléopâtre s'en aperçut incontinent* . . .

(c) On a time he went to angle for fish, and when he could take none, he was as angry *as could be*, bicause Cleopatra stoode by. Wherefore he secretly commanded the fisher men that, *when he cast in his line*, they should *straight* dive under the water, and put a fishe on his hooke which they had taken before; and so *snatched up* his angling rodde and *brought up* fish twice or thrice. Cleopatra found it *straight* . . .

(d) We see here again some expansions, which make the anecdote more diffuse. North is not slavish: he omits Amyot's *voyant que* in the first sentence, and has his own way of duplicating the idea of 'anger'—'as angry as could be' for *fort dépit et marri*. The most significant feature however is the treatment of the sentence-structure. Plutarch's period consists of (i) a 'when' clause, down to 'was present'; (ii) a main sentence with two coordinate verbs, 'ordered' and 'did-not-escape-notice (*ouk elathe*)'. The translators break the period up: a normal procedure for them—and, *mutatis mutandis*, for modern translators too. The final phrase is idiomatic in Greek and presents a small problem; Amyot very naturally made a separate point of it and (as we shall see) connected it with the next period.

6. (a) Pretending to be astonished, she told her friends and invited them to be spectators the following day.

(b) . . . toutefois elle fit semblant *de n'en rien savoir*, et de s'émerveiller *comment il pêchait si bien*; mais *à part* elle conta *le tour* à ses familiers, et leur dit que le lendemain il se trouvassent *sur l'eau* pour voir *l'ébattement*.

(c) . . . yet she seemed not *to see it*, *but* wondred *at his excellent fishing*: but *when she was alone by herself among* her owne people, she told them *how it was*, and bad them the next morning *to be on the water* to see *the fishing*.

(d) The situation has been clarified by making a clear separation in time between Cleopatra's pretended admiration and her subsequent invitation to her friends. At the same time, a good deal of vivid detail has been added: we seem to hear what she said—or what might have been said in a fishing invitation at the court of Henri II. Plutarch does not dwell on this part of the story; he needs to get on.

7. (*a*) Many having embarked on the fishing boats and Antony having let down his tackle, she ordered one of her men to get there first and swim up to the hook and fasten on it a piece of Pontic dried fish.

(*b*) Ils y *vinrent sur le port* en grande nombre, et se mirent dans des bateaux de pêcheurs, et Antoine aussi lâcha sa ligne, et *lors* Cléopâtre commanda à l'un de ses serviteurs qu'il se hâtât de plonger devant ceux d'Antoine, et qu'il allât attacher à l'hameçon *de sa ligne* quelque vieux poisson salé, comme *ceux que l'on apporte du pays de Pont.*

(*c*) A number of people *came to the haven*, and got into the fisher boates *to see this fishing.* Antonius then threw in his line and *Cleopatra straight* commanded one of her men to dive under water before Antonius men, and to put some olde salte fishe upon his baite, *like unto those that are brought out of the contrie of Pont.*

(*d*) Once again, the period is dissolved and details are added (*sur le port*); North expands here and there even where Amyot does not. We also have an explanatory addition, the sort of thing that a modern translator would put in a footnote: Pontus (i.e. the Black Sea or its southern coast) was famous for dried fish. Amyot clearly thought that Cleopatra's piece of fish was not actually from Pontus, only that sort of thing; he need not be right about this.

8. (*a*) When, convinced that he had a bite, Antony pulled in, laughter breaking out (as one might expect [*eikos*]), she said 'Give over the rod, general, to us kings in Pharos and Canobos; your hunting (*thēra*) is cities and kingdoms and continents.'

(*b*) Cela fait, Antoine, qui cuida qu'il y eût un poisson pris, tira *incontinent* sa ligne; et adonc, comme l'on peut penser, *tous les assistants* prirent bien fort à rire, et Cléopâtre *en riant* lui dit: 'Laisse-nous, seigneur, à nous autres Égyptiens *habitants* de Pharus et de Canopus, laisse-nous la ligne; *ce n'est pas ton métier*; ta chasse est *de prendre et de conquérir* villes *et cités, pays et royaumes.*

(c) *When he had hong the fish on his hooke,* Antonius thinking he had taken a fishe *in deede,* snatched up his line *presently.* Then they all fell a laughing. Cleopatra *laughing also* said unto him: 'Leave us (my Lord) Aegyptians (which *dwell* in the country of Pharus and Canobus) your angle rodde: *this is not thy profession*: thou must hunt after conquering of *realms and contries.*'

(d) This passage is the culmination of the story, because it leads to Cleopatra's apophthegm. The translators have again made some changes. (*i*) The addition of *incontinent*, 'straight', serves as often to indicate a relationship in time which is not in the Greek: cf. the same words in 5, and *lors* in 7. (*ii*) Cleopatra laughs as well as everybody else. (*iii*) Amyot evidently did not accept the manuscript reading '*Kings* of Pharos and Canobos.' (*iv*) *Ce n'est pas ton métier* is added. (*v*) The rhetorical point of the last sentence is marred both by the expansion of *thēra* (chase, game) and by the duplication of 'cities' and 'kingdoms' coupled with the omission of the climactic word 'continents', which makes a special point: Antony was lord of Asia and Africa, and could be lord of Europe.

Such was the Plutarch that Shakespeare knew. The differences from the real Plutarch may well be reckoned pure gain; but they are distortions none the less, and it is well to grasp the nature of them if we are to understand either Plutarch or the Elizabethans.

CHAPTER TEN

Conclusion

THE two centuries following the age of the great translators mark the peak of Plutarch's influence on Western civilisation. To put it more precisely, they mark the widest diffusion of the notion of antiquity and its values that the Renaissance had constructed, and for this notion Plutarch was, as he had been in the late empire, a central and inescapable text-book. Racine at the age of sixteen read all the *Lives* and *Moralia* and made notes on the moral—and even theological—lessons to be drawn from them.[1] An exceptional boy in an exceptional school; but thousands will have been led in the same paths.

The great translations themselves, despite refurbishing,[2] soon fell into disrepute, ostensibly because of their inaccuracies, but largely because changes in vernacular style had made them quaint and ridiculous. Translation is among the most ephemeral of literary arts. Dryden in 1683, introducing a collaborative version of the *Lives* to which he lent his name, alludes to North as 'our old English translation' without so much as naming him. Holland's *Moralia* was superseded at the same time by a generous selection done by a group of scholars, mainly from Oxford. Matthew Morgan, of St. John's, wrote the Preface:

As for our countryman, Dr. Holland, it must be allowed him that he understood Greek . . . His Pegasus was of the true Northern strain, it

---

[1] In the *Pléiade Racine*, II 934 ff. Note for example his instance of the vice of curiosity: 'ne regarder pas en monastère de filles.'
[2] Amyot was superficially modernised and supplied with fresh moral annotation by Simon Goulart.

serv'd to carry him out of the Dirt and bring him to his Journey's end
with an heavy Trot.[3]

Both these new versions had a long life. 'Dryden's' Lives were
revised in Victorian times by A. H. Clough, and have probably
been more widely read than either North or the later and duller
work of the Langhorne brothers (1770). The *Morals* by 'Several
Hands' also had a nineteenth-century revision, and much im-
pressed and influenced Emerson.[4]

There is a passage in Dryden's Life of Plutarch—which was
largely but not altogether based on Rualdus (1624)—which
provokes reflection. He is in effect considering the relation
between style and content:

In Plutarch, whose business was not to please the ear but to charm and
to instruct the mind, we may easily forgive the cadences of words and
the roughness of expression. Yet, for manliness of eloquence, if it
abounded not in our author, it was not wanting in him. He neither
studied the sublime style, nor affected the flowery. The choice of
words, the numbers of periods, the turns of sentences, and those other
ornaments of speech, he neither sought nor shunned; but the depth of
sense, the accuracy of judgment, the disposition of the parts, and
contexture of the whole, in so admirable and vast a field of matter, and
lastly the copiousness and variety of words, appear shining in our
author.

Now this is for the most part quite untrue. It is based on the
classical doctrine of types of style; if Plutarch has neither the
'sublime' nor the 'flowery', it follows by elimination that he has
the 'plain'. No reader of Plutarch could easily think that. To deny
that he seeks rhythmical periods and rhetorical ornament is
another falsehood. To commend his 'disposition' is to praise
where praise is least due. But, wide of the mark as this criticism
is, it nevertheless became in a sense the standard one. In place
of the essayist Plutarch of the sixteenth century, we have the plain
man who puts meaning before style, and teaches plain sense in a

[3] In Pope's *Dunciad* (1.134), 'the groaning shelves Philemon bends', among
solid volumes of an earlier age.
[4] E. G. Berry, *Actes du VIII*^e *Congrès . . . Budé*, 578 ff.

workmanlike and undistinguished dress. Erasmus and Amyot—and indeed Matthew Morgan—knew better. The consequences of this view were serious. In emphasising the message to the exclusion of the verbal form, it made Plutarch's reputation rest on the acceptability of his opinions, and left no room for a strictly literary judgment. It thus prepared the way for the depreciation in his stock that came in the nineteenth century. There were two main causes of this depreciation: one was the growing historical consciousness that was scandalised by Plutarch's neglect of the differences between one age and another and at the moralistic presuppositions of his scholarship; the other was the obsolescence, in the world of modern Europe, of many of the values which he enshrined. It is not always easy to distinguish these points. Both, for example, seem to be implied in the spiced sentences of Macaulay:

> The heroes of Livy are the most insipid of all beings, real or imaginary, the heroes of Plutarch always excepted. Indeed, the manner of Plutarch in this respect reminds us of the cookery of those continental inns, the horror of English travellers, in which a certain nondescript broth is kept constantly boiling, and copiously poured, without distinction, over every dish as it comes up to table.[5]

It seems at any rate to be generally true that Plutarch ceased, in the course of the nineteenth century, to have the enormous influence over active minds which he had had down to the age of Rousseau and Benjamin Franklin. It is true that one can find evidence enough of him in very diverse literary men: an Emerson or a Thomas Mann.[6] And in practical men too: are we not told that General Gordon recommended the *Lives* as a handbook for young officers? But on the whole schoolboys and scholars have succeeded the princes and philosophers and ladies of the court as Plutarch's typical readers. And in education, at least in England, he suffered from a drawback not felt since the time of the Atticist

---

[5] 'History' (*Edinburgh Review*, 1828; printed in all editions of *Essays*). For the culinary image, compare Macaulay's celebrated comparison of Seneca to 'anchovy sauce'.

[6] See the Introduction to T. J. Reed's ed. of *Tod in Venedig*, Oxford 1971.

grammarians: the extreme classicism of Greek studies. He was no model for prose. Scholarship, for its part, was by now predominantly historical. This led to an enormous effort to trace Plutarch's 'sources', whether in history or in philosophy. *Quellenkritik* is a necessary tool in the exploration of the ancient world. Its danger lies in the temptation to neglect the purposes and procedures of the authors who transmit the tradition. With a writer of Plutarch's sophistication, the risks are obvious. During the past half century or so—say, since Friedrich Leo's book on Greek and Roman biography (1901)—much has been done to clarify and avoid them. But much remains. Linguistic and stylistic studies of Plutarch are not numerous; one inhibiting factor is the absence of a lexicon subsequent to the one by Daniel Wyttenbach, published posthumously (1830) out of the interleaved Index to Aelian in which that great scholar had written the entries. And beyond the linguistic investigation is the question of a fresh literary evaluation. In writing this book, I have tried to make a provisional contribution in this direction, and I conclude by trying to define the problem a little more clearly.

When we read a classical poet who has been thoroughly studied —let us say Horace—we have to 'learn the language' in a special sense: to accumulate and master a very large amount of information about the details of a literary tradition. Only when this has been done are we in a position to estimate what Horace's achievement is, to read him as scholars, or to explain him to others. And it is not only the detail of the tradition but its nature that matters: we have above all to bear constantly in mind the difficult truth that ancient writers think of their work primarily in terms of persuasive presentation. The reference to the audience determines almost everything, the reference to the author or the subject comparatively little. Thus in reading poetry we have to move away from the notion that the poet is 'expressing himself'. An analogous situation arises even in informative literature—in Plutarch, say, or in the philosophical works of Cicero. We have to remember that the philosopher and the historian are also presenting a case and not putting down the facts without regard to the audience.

Plutarch, as we have seen, is, in almost every one of his works, the conscious artist, deploying a full repertoire of rhetorical techniques and controlling an exceptionally rich and allusive language. The purpose of the *opus musaicum* is to convince, even if it is not so much by logic as by a display of brilliance and erudition.

The relation between the rhetoric and the conceptual content in such a writer is not an easy one to define. Perhaps we can do it best by pointing out some obviously different cases. Plotinus is one extreme, a writer struggling with difficult thought and generally indifferent to rhetorical presentation. Maximus of Tyre is the other, a rhetor playing with philosophy or science for amusement. Plutarch and Cicero fall somewhere between; in principle, they subordinate literary techniques to instructional ends, but in practice the imagery and the rhetoric come near to being an end in themselves. It is all a little like didactic poetry. Similarly, in history, we can read Polybius as a statesmanlike record of political activity; at the other end of the scale, we can see that Herodian is merely using events as a framework for a display of speeches and set descriptions. The *Lives*, again, fall somewhere between, as indeed does most ancient historical writing. Just what the relation between form and content is in any individual Life, or indeed any individual passage, is a matter for detailed analysis and commentary. There is no short cut. In the passages I have quoted and discussed in the course of this book I have tried to show how I think this may be attempted, what complexities and what simplicities we may expect: in a word, what it is like to read Plutarch.

Appendix

I give here:

   (i) a list of the works in the *Moralia*, in the traditional order;
  (ii) a list of the Lives;
 (iii) a note on editions and translations which include all or much of Plutarch;
 (iv) some important general books on Plutarch.

This list is of course very selective. It does not include all the works referred to in the footnotes.

(*i*) LIST OF WORKS IN THE MORALIA

The order and pagination of the extant books are taken from the Frankfurt edition of 1599 (Greek with Xylander's Latin) which modern editions almost all follow. I have given each book an English title, and have used this in the text. The conventional Greek titles which follow are probably not Plutarch's own; the Latin titles vary somewhat in different editions. A brief note on separate editions and commentaries is appended, and some references to books listed under (iv) and to some early Latin and English translations.*
Compare the list prefixed to each volume of the Loeb *Moralia*. For the 'Lamprias Catalogue', see above, p. 18, it is published in vol. xv of the Loeb edition.

[1] 1A–14C   The Education of Children (*Peri paidōn agōgēs, De liberis educandis*)
                     Spurious (Wyttenbach, Animadversiones, I, 29 ff.): a very influential book in Renaissance educational writing (Aeneas Sylvius, Melanchthon, Milton, Rousseau). Latin: Guarino (printed 1471). English: Sir T. Elyot, 1532.

2. 14D–37B.   On Reading the Poets (*Pōs dei ton neon poiēmatōn akouein, Quomodo adulescens poetas audire debeat (De audiendis poetis)*)
                     Lamprias Catalogue 103. Above, pp. 51 ff.

* For further details, and translations into other languages, see R. Aulotte, *Amyot et Plutarque*, 325–51.

3. 37C–48D.   On Listening to Lectures (*Peri tou akouein, De recta ratione audiendi*)
Lamprias Catalogue 102.

4. 48E–74E.   Friends and Flatterers (*Pōs an tis diakrineie ton kolaka tou philou, Quomodo adulator ab amico internoscatur (De adulatore et amico)*)
Lamprias Catalogue 89. Above, pp. 94 ff. Latin: Guarino 1437; Erasmus 1514.

5. 75A–86A.   Progress in Virtue (*Pōs an tis aisthoito heautou prokoptontos ep' aretēi, Quomodo quis suas in virtute sentiat profectus (De profectibus in virtute)*)
Lamprias Catalogue 87. Above, p. 87 f. Babut, 47 ff. Latin: Erasmus 1514, R. Pace 1511–14. English: anon. 1535.

6. 86B–92E.   How to Profit from Your Enemies (*Pōs an tis ap' echthrōn ōpheloito, De capienda ex inimicis utilitate*)
Lamprias Catalogue 130. Above, p. 96 f. Latin: Cincius Romanus c. 1440.

7. 93A–97B.   On Having Many Friends (*Peri poluphilias, De amicorum multitudine*)
Above, p. 93 f.

8. 97C–100A.   Fortune (*Peri tuchēs, De fortuna*)
Incomplete; declamatory in manner.

9. 100A–101D.   Virtue and Vice (*Peri aretēs kai kakias, De virtute et vitio*)
Incomplete; declamatory in manner.

[10] 101E–121D.   Consolation to Apollonius (*Paramuthētikos pros Apollōnion, Consolatio ad Apollonium*)
Spurious; a useful collection of consolatory commonplaces. Commentary in R. Kassel, *Untersuchungen zur griechischen und römischen Konsolationsliteratur*, 1958.

11. 122B–137E.   Advice on Health (*Hugieina parangelmata, De tuenda sanitate praecepta*)
Lamprias Catalogue 94. Latin: Erasmus 1514. English: R. Wyer 1530; J. Hales 1543.

12. 138A–146A.   Advice on Marriage (*Gamika parangelmata, Coniugalia praecepta*)
Lamprias Catalogue 115. Above, p. 90 f. cf. Jeremy

Taylor, *Eniautos*, part 1, sermon 17, 'The Marriage Ring'.

13. 146B–164D. The Banquet of the Seven Sages (*Tōn hepta sophōn sumposion, Septem sapientium convivium*) Lamprias Catalogue 110. Above, p. 35 f. Ed. J. Defradas, Paris 1954.

14. 164E–171E. Superstition (*Peri deisidaimonias, De superstitione*) Lamprias Catalogue 155. Above, p. 79 f. Latin: J. Cheke, dedicated to Henry VIII, but not printed till 1552.

[15] 172A–208A. Sayings of Kings and Commanders (*Basileōn apophthegmata kai stratēgōn, Regum et imperatorum apophthegmata*) Lamprias Catalogue 108, 125. Preface is forged, and the whole work spurious, even if it uses Plutarch's material. Erasmus' Latin adaptation 1531; English version by N. Udall 1540.

[16] 208A–242D. Spartan Sayings (*Apophthegmata Lakōnika, Apothegmata Laconica.* Lamprias Catalogue 169.

17. 242E–263C. Brave Deeds of Women (*Gunaikōn aretai, Mulierum virtutes*) Lamprias Catalogue 126, ?167. P. A. Stadter, *Plutarch's Historical Methods*, Harvard 1965.

18. 263D–291C, 291D–304F. Roman Questions, Greek Questions (*Aitia Rōmaïka, Aitia Hellēnika, Quaestiones Romanae, Quaestiones Graecae*) Lamprias Catalogue 138. Roman Question: H. J. Rose, Oxford 1924 (trans. and commentary). Greek Questions: W. R. Halliday, Oxford 1928 (trans. and commentary).

[19] 305A–316B. Minor Parallels (*Sunagōgē historiōn parallēlōn Hellēnikōn kai Rōmaiōn₁ Parallela minora*) Spurious.

20. 316B–326C. The Fortune of the Romans (*Peri tēs Romaiōn tuchēs, De fortuna Romanorum*) Lamprias Catalogue 175. Above, p. 131. Latin: J. Angeli da Scarperia (?), *d.* 1411.

21. 326D–345B. Fortune and Virtue in Alexander the Great, 1–2 (*Peri*

tēs Alexandrou tuchēs ē aretēs, i–ii, De Alexandri magni fortuna aut virtute, i–ii)
Lamprias Catalogue 176, 186. J. R. Hamilton, *Plutarch's Alexander*, Introd. xxiii–xxxiii.

22. 345D–351B. The Glory of Athens (*Poteron Athēnaioi kata polemon ē kata sophian endoxoteroi, Bellone an pace clariores fuerint Athenienses (De gloria Atheniensium)*)
Lamprias Catalogue 197 (?) Above, pp. 31 ff.

23. 351C–384C. Isis and Osiris (*Peri Isidos kai Osiridos, De Iside et Osiride*)
Lamprias Catalogue 118. Above, pp. 75, 82 f. J. Gwyn Griffith, ed. with trans. and commentary, University of Wales Press, 1970.

24. 384D–394C. The Delphic 'E' (*Peri tou E tou en Delphois, De E apud Delphos*)
Lamprias Catalogue 117. Ed. R. Flacelière, Paris 1941.

25. 394D–409D. The Pythia's Prophecies (*Peri tou mē chran emmetra nūn tēn Puthian* (i.e. 'on the fact that the Pythia does not now prophesy in verse'), *De Pythiae oraculis*)
Lamprias Catalogue 116. Above, pp. 15 ff. Ed. R. Flacelière, Paris 1937 (also 1962, in *Collection Erasme*, without translation).

26. 409E–438E. The decline of Oracles (*Peri tōn ekleloipotōn chrēstēriōn, De defectu oraculorum*)
Lamprias Catalogue 88. Above, p. 75. Ed. R. Flacelière, Paris 1947.

27. 439A–440C. Is Virtue Teachable? (*Ei didakton hē aretē, An virtus doceri possit*
Lamprias Catalogue 180. Incomplete; declamatory.

28. 440C–452D. Moral Virtue (*Peri ēthikēs aretēs, De virtute morali*)
Lamprias Catalogue 72. Above, pp. 84 f. Ed. D. Babut, Paris 1969.

29. 452E–464D. The Control of Anger (*Peri aorgēsias, De cohibenda ira*)
D. A. Russell, 'On Reading Plutarch's Moralia', *Greece and Rome*; 1966. Above, p. 11. H. G. Ingenkamp, *Plutarchs Schriften über die Heilung der Seele*, 1971, 14 ff. Latin: Simon Altumanus 1373; Coluccio Salutati, before 1406; Erasmus 1526; W. Pirckheimer 1526.

30. 464E–477F.   Quiet of Mind (*Peri euthumias, De tranquillitate animi*) Lamprias Catalogue 95. Above, pp. 23 ff. H. Broecker, *Animadversiones* . . ., Bonn 1954 (commentary, in Latin). Latin: G. Budé 1505. English: Sir T. Wyatt 1528.

31. 478A–492D.   Brotherly Love (*Peri philadelphias, De fraterno amore*) Lamprias Catalogue 98. Above, p. 9.

32. 493A–497E.   Love of offspring (*Peri tēs eis ta ekgona philostorgias, De amore prolis*) Declamatory; incomplete or unfinished.

33. 498A–500A.   Is Vice a Sufficient Cause of Misery? (*Ei autarkēs hē kakia pros kakodaimonian, An vitiositas ad infelicitatem sufficiat*) Declamatory; incomplete.

34. 500B–502D.   Ills of the Body and Ills of the Mind (*Peri tou poteron ta psuchēs ē ta sōmatos pathē cheirona, Animine an corporis affectiones sint peiores*) Declamatory; fragmentary.

35. 502B–515A.   Talkativeness (*Peri adoleschias, De garrulitate*) Lamprias Catalogue 92. Ingenkamp, op. cit., 26 ff. Latin: R. Pace 1522; W. Pirckheimer 1523.

36. 515B–523B.   Curiosity (*Peri polupragmosunēs, De curiositate*) Lamprias Catalogue 97. Above, p. 88. Ingenkamp, 44 ff. Latin: W. Pirckheimer 1523; Erasmus 1526. English: Queen Elizabeth I (1598), (ed. Caroline Pemberton, London 1899).

37. 523C–528B.   Love of Money (*Peri philoploutias, De cupiditate divitiarum*) Lamprias Catalogue 211. Cf. the fragments of another work on a similar theme, fr. 149–52 Sandbach. Latin: Erasmus 1514; R. Pace 1522.

38. 528C–536D.   Harmful Scrupulousness (*Peri dusōpias, De vitioso pudore*) Lamprias Catalogue 96. Above, p. 89. Ingenkamp 54 ff. Latin: Erasmus 1526.

39. 536D–538E.   Envy and Hatred (*Peri phthonou kai misous, De invidia et odio*) Fragmentary.

40. 539A–547F. Self-Praise without Offence (*Peri tou heauton epainein anepiphthonōs, De laude ipsius*)
Lamprias Catalogue 85. Ingenkamp 62 ff.

41. 548A–568A. God's Slowness to Punish (*Peri tōn tou theiou bradeōs timōroumenōn, De sera numinis vindicta*)
Lamprias Catalogue 91. Above, p. 85. Commentary by Wyttenbach. Cf. Jeremy Taylor, *The Descending and Entailed Curse Cut Off* (vol. 4.361–9, ed. Heber-Eden); *The Faith and Patience of the Saints* (vol. 4, 453–69). Latin: W. Pirckheimer 1513.

[42] 568B–574F. Fate (*Peri heimarmenēs, De fato*)
? = Lamprias Catalogue 58 (though this refers to *two* books on Fate). Spurious: a 'middle Platonist' work of some historical importance.

43. 575A–598F. Socrates' Sign (*Peri tou Sōkratous daimoniou, De genio Socratis*)
Lamprias Catalogue 69. Above, pp. 36 ff. Ed. A. Corlu Paris 1970.

44. 599A–607F. Exile (*Peri phugēs, De exilio*)
Lamprias Catalogue 101.

45. 608A–612A. Consolation to My Wife (*Paramuthētikos pros tēn gunaika, Consolatio ad uxorem*)
Lamprias Catalogue 112. Above, pp. 5, 78.

46. 612C–748D. Table Talk, I–IX (*Sumposiakōn biblia ennea, Quaestionum Convivalium libri ix*)
Above, pp. 5, 44.

47. 748E–711E. A Book of Love (*Erōtikos, Amatorius*)
Lamprias Catalogue 107. Above, pp. 5, 35, 92.

[48] 771E–775E. Love Stories (*Erōtikai diēgēseis, Amatoriae narrationes*)
Apparently = Lamprias Catalogue 222; but certainly spurious. Latin: Politian 1479.

49. 776A–779C. Philosophers and Princes (*Peri tou hoti malista tois hēgemosi dei ton philosophon dialegesthai, Maxime cum principibus philosopho esse disserendum*)
Fragmentary. Latin: Erasmus 1514.

50. 779D–782F. The Uneducated Prince (*Pros hēgemona apaideuton, Ad principem ineruditum*)
Declamatory; fragmentary. Latin: Erasmus 1514.

51. 783A–797F. Old Men in Politics (*Ei presbuterōi politeuteon, An seni sit gerenda res publica*) Lamprias Catalogue 75.

52. 798A–825F. Advice on Public Life (*Politika parangelmata, Praecepta gerendae reipublicae*) Lamprias Catalogue 104. Above, p. 97 f. T. Renoirté, *Les Conseils politiques de Plutarque*, Louvain 1950.

53. 826A–827C. Monarchy, Democracy, and Oligarchy (*Peri monarchias kai dēmokratias kai oligarchias, De unius in republica dominatione, populari statu, et paucorum imperio*) Incomplete.

54. 827D–832A. Do Not Borrow! (*Peri tou mē dein daneizesthai, De vitando aere alieno*) Lamprias Catalogue 215. Above, pp. 29 ff. Latin. W. Pirckheimer 1515.

[55] 832B–852C. Lives of the Ten Orators (*Bioi tōn deka rhētorōn, Vitae decem oratorum*) Spurious; an important source for ancient knowledge of the Attic orators from Antiphon to Dinarchus.

56. 853A–854D. Comparison of Aristophanes and Menander (abridgement) (*Sunkriseōs Aristophanous kai Menandrou epitomē, Comparationis Aristophanis et Menandri compendium*) cf. above, p. 53.

57. 854E–874C. Herodotus' Malice (*Peri tēs Hērodotou kakoētheias, De Herodoti malignitate*) Above, pp. 60 ff.

[58] 874A–911C. Doctrines of the Philosophers (*Peri tōn areskontōn philosophois phusikōn dogmatōn, De placitis philosophorum*) Five books; not Plutarch's own work. An important source-book: cf. H. Diels, *Doxographi Graeci* (1879), for the fundamental discussion and parallel texts.

59. 911C–919E. Natural Questions (*Aitia phusika, Quaestiones naturales*) Lamprias Catalogue 218. Incompletely preserved.

60. 920A–945E. The Face in the Moon (*Peri tou emphainomenou prosōpou tōi kuklōi tēs selēnēs, De facie (quae) in orbe lunae (apparet)*) Lamprias Catalogue 73. Above, pp. 69 ff. Ed. P. Raingeard, Paris 1935 (of little use); but H. Cherniss in Loeb vol. XII offers a substantial and valuable commentary; the astronomer J. Kepler also composed a Latin

translation and commentary, which is still of great interest.

61. 945F–955F. The Primary Cold (*Peri tou prōtōs psuchrou, De primo frigido*) Lamprias Catalogue 90.

62. 955D–958E. Which is More Useful, Fire or Water? (*Poteron hudōr ē pūr chrēsimōteron, Aquane an ignis sit utilior*) Declamatory; authenticity suspected.

63. 959A–985C. The Intelligence of Animals (*Potera tōn ʒōōn phronimōtera, ta chersaia ē ta enudra, Terrestriane an aquatilia animalia sint callidiora* (*De sollertia animalium*) Above, pp. 13 ff.

64. 985D–992E. Gryllus (*Peri tou ta aloga logōi chrēsthai, Bruta animalia ratione uti* (*Gryllus*)) Lamprias Catalogue 127.

64–66. 993A–999B. On Eating Flesh, 1–2 (*Peri sarkophagias i–ii, De esu carnium i–ii*) Two speeches; incompletely and badly preserved.

67. 999C–1011F. Platonic Questions (*Platōnika ʒētēmata, Platonicae Quaestiones*) Lamprias Catalogue 136.

68. 1012A–30C. The Creation of the Soul in Plato's 'Timaeus' (*Peri tēs en Timaiōi psuchogonias, De animae procreatione in Timaeo*) Lamprias Catalogue 65. Above, pp. 65 ff.

69. 1030D–1032F. Epitome of 68.

70. 1033A–1057C. Contradictions of the Stoics (*Peri Stōikōn enantiōmatōn, De Stoicorum repugnantiis*) Lamprias Catalogue 76. Above, p. 68. On this, and the other anti-stoic works, see especially D. Babut, *Plutarque et le stoicisme*.

71. 1057C–1058D. Stoic Paradoxes Are Stranger than Poets' (*Hoti paradoxotera hoi Stōikoi tōn poiētōn legousin, Stoicos absurdiora poetis dicere*) Lamprias Catalogue 79. Declamatory; incomplete.

72. 1058E–1086B. Common Notions: Against the Stoic View (*Peri tōn koinōn ennoiōn pros tous Stōikous, De communibus notitiis adversus Stoicos*) Lamprias Catalogue 77.

73. 1086C–1107C. Not Even a Pleasant Life is Possible on Epicurean

Principles (*Hoti oud'hēdeōs ʒēn estin kat' Epikouron*, *Non posse suaviter vivi secundum Epicurum*) Above, p. 67.

74. 1107D–1127E. Against Colotes (*Pros Kōlōten*, *Adversus Colotem*) Lamprias Catalogue 81. Above, p. 68. R. Westman, *Acta Philosophica Fennica*, VII, 1955.

75. 1128A–1130C. The Unnoticed Life (*Ei kalōs eirētai to 'lathe biōsas'*, *An recte dictum sit latenter esse vivendum* (*De latenter vivendo*)) Lamprias Catalogue 178. Declamatory.

[76] 1131A–1147A. Music (*Peri mousikēs*, *De musica*) A history in a dialogue setting: not by Plutarch. Ed. F. Lasserre, Lausanne 1954.

[77–8] Two brief pieces on (*i*) whether desire and grief are psychical or somatic phenomena, (*ii*) whether the affective element in man should be regarded as a part or a faculty of his soul. These were first published by T. Tyrwhitt from a Harleian MS in 1773, in which they are attributed to Plutarch. They do not seem to be his: v. Sandbach, Loeb *Moralia* XV, 32–7.

Fragments. These are collected by F. H. Sandbach (*i*) in the Teubner *Moralia*, vol. VII; (*ii*) in the Loeb, vol. XV, *Spuria*. Three other works often published with Plutarch's works (last in Bernardakis' Teubner edition, vol. VII, 1896) should be mentioned. (*i*) *Nobility* was first published in a Latin version in 1556, the Greek text only in 1724; it is probably a late Byzantine forgery.

(*ii*) *The Life and Poetry of Homer* is an important source for ancient allegorical and other interpretations of Homer; it was included in the Plutarch corpus known to Planudes. (*iii*) *On Rivers* is a 'book of wonders' preserved in a single manuscript. Other *spuria* are of less general interest; they are to be found in Bernardakis' edition. New editions are needed.

(*ii*) LIST OF THE LIVES

The order of the Lives varies in the manuscripts and in printed editions, while the 'Lamprias Catalogue' shows traces of a different arrangement again. The following list follows the 'tripartite recension', adopted in the Teubner edition; but I have added volume-references to the Loeb and the Budé. A few separate commentaries have been mentioned; there is a vast literature on the Lives, mainly historical, to which I have made little or no reference here. The Budé introductions, where they exist, should be consulted.

I.1

Theseus and Romulus (Loeb I, Budé I)
Solon and Publicola (Loeb I, Budé II)
Themistocles and Camillus (Loeb II, Budé II)
  Themistocles: ed. F. Blass 1872; A. Bauer 1884; H. A. Holden³ 1892.
Aristides and Cato Maior (Loeb II, Budé V)
  Ed. F. Blass, 1872. *Aristides*: ed. I. C. Limentani, Florence 1964.
Cimon and Lucullus (Loeb II)

I.2

Pericles and Fabius Maximus (Loeb III, Budé III)
  Pericles: ed. F. Blass 1872; H. A. Holden, 1894; cf. E. Meinhardt, *Perikles bei Plutarch*, Frankfurt 1957.
Nicias and Crassus (Loeb III)
  Nicias: ed. H. A. Holden, 1887.
Coriolanus and Alcibiades (Loeb IV, Budé III)
  cf. above, chaps. 6–7.
Demosthenes and Cicero (Loeb VII)
  Demosthenes: ed. H. A. Holden, 1893. *Cicero*: ed. D. Magnino, Florence, 1962.

II.1

Phocion and Cato Minor (Loeb VIII)
Dion and Brutus (Loeb VI)
  Dion: ed. W. H. Porter, Dublin 1952. *Brutus*: ed. R. del Re, Florence 1948.
Aemilius Paulus and Timoleon (Loeb VI, Budé IV)
  Aemilius: ed. Ch. Liedmeier, Nijmegen 1937; A. Witlox, Zwolle 1937.
  Timoleon: ed. O. Siefert—F. Blass, 1879; ed. H. A. Holden, 1889.
Sertorius and Eumenes (Loeb VIII)

II.2

Philopoemen and Flamininus (Loeb X, Budé V)
    Ed. O. Siefert—G. Blass, 1876.
Pelopidas and Marcellus (Loeb V, Budé IV)
Alexander and Caesar (Loeb VII)
    Alexander: ed. J. R. Hamilton, Oxford 1969. *Caesar*: ed. A. Garzetti,
        Florence 1954.

III.1

Demetrius and Antony (Loeb IX)
    Demetrius: ed. E. Manni, Florence 1953. *Antony*: cf. above, pp. 169 ff.
Pyrrhus and Marius (Loeb IX, Budé VI)
    Pyrrhus: ed. O. Siefert—F. Blass, 1879; A. B. Nederlof, Amsterdam 1940.
    Marius: ed. E. Valgiglio, Florence 1965.
Aratus (Loeb XI)
    Ed. W. H. Porter 1937.
Artaxerxes (Loeb XI)
Agis and Cleomenes: *T. and C. Gracchus* (Loeb X)
    Ed. F. Blass, 1875. *Gracchi*: ed. H. A. Holden, 1885; ed. E. Valgiglio, 1963.

III.2

Lycurgus and Numa (Loeb I, Budé I)
Lysander and Sulla (Loeb IV, Budé VI)
    Sulla: ed. H. A. Holden, 1886.
Agesilaus and Pompeius (Loeb V)
Galba and Otho (Loeb XI)
    Ed. E. G. Hardy, 1890.

(*iii*) EDITIONS AND TRANSLATIONS

EDITIONS

The standard modern editions of the *Moralia* are (*i*) the Loeb, by various hands, in 15 vols.; a change of policy after vol. 6 makes the later volumes very much more informative and scholarly; (*ii*) the Teubner, initiated by a group of scholars inspired by Wilamowitz, and not yet quite complete after more than fifty years; this is the essential edition, both for textual information and for parallels and cross-references in other authors. A Budé edition is planned, and has begun to appear. Of older editions, D. Wyttenbach's (1795–1830) retains its value for its commentary (incomplete) and lexicon (imperfect, but not yet replaced).

For the *Lives*, Loeb (B. Perrin) and Teubner (C. Lindskog—K. Ziegler) provide similar services again, though the Loeb does not have so much annotation here as in the latter part of the *Moralia*. The Budé edition (R. Flacelière), with French translation, is still incomplete. It combines a good text with excellent introductions to each life.

TRANSLATIONS

Moralia

For a list of sixteenth-century versions, Latin and vernacular, see R. Aulotte, *Amyot et Plutarque*, Geneva 1965, 325 ff.: see also his *Plutarque en France au XVIe siècle*, Paris 1971.

Philemon Holland's translation (1603, 1657) has not been reprinted in its entirety: but there is a selection, ed. E. H. Blakeney, in Dent's Everyman's Library (1912).

The seventeenth-century version 'by several hands' (1684–94) was reissued, revised by W. W. Goodwin, in the last century (1874–8). Modern selections in translation include the volumes by C. W. King and A. R. Shilleto (Bohn Library), T. G. Tucker and A. O. Prickard (Oxford, 1913 and 1918), and Rex Warner (Penguin, 1971).

Lives

There is an excellent annotated reprint of Amyot by G. Walter, Bibliothèque de la Pléiade, 1951. North has fared well for reprints: e.g. ed. G. Wyndham, Tudor Translations, 1895; selections illustrating Shakespeare in T. J. B. Spencer, *Shakespeare's Plutarch*, Penguin Books 1964; or (with fuller comment) in G. Bullough, *Narrative and Dramatic Sources of Shakespeare*, vols. v and vi, 1964. The translation prefaced by Dryden (1683–6) has often been reprinted, especially as revised by A. H. Clough (e.g. Everyman Library). The Langhorne brothers' version (1770) and that by Stewart and Long (Bohn, 1880–2) are the principal later translations. Twenty-seven Lives are available in Penguin Classics by Ian Scott-Kilvert (three vols.—*The Rise and Fall of Athens, Makers of Rome, The Fall of the Roman Republic*).

(*iv*) GENERAL BIBLIOGRAPHY

Actes du VIIIe Congrès de l'Association Guillaume Budé, Paris, 1969, 481–594 (includes report on recent work, by R. Flacelière).

R. Aulotte, *Amyot et Plutarque*, Geneva 1965.
[Very valuable and important]

D. Babut, *Plutarque et le stoïcisme*, Paris 1969.
[Detailed, and wider in range than the title suggests]

N. I. Barbu, *Les Procédés de la peinture des caractères et la vérité historique dans les biographies de Plutarque*, Paris 1934.
[Not satisfactory, but still the only long treatment of the subject]

R. H. Barrow, *Plutarch and His Times*, London 1967.

A. Dihle, *Studien zur griechischen Biographie*, Gottingen 1956.

O. Gréard, *De la morale de Plutarque*, Paris 1866.
[Stimulating and wise in its approach]

J. J. Hartman, *De Avondzon des Heidendoms*, Leiden³, 1924.
[A highly personal book by a lifelong enthusiast]

W. C. Helmbold & E. N. O'Neil, *Plutarch's Quotations*, American Philological Association, 1959.

R. Hirzel, *Der Dialog*, Leipzig 1895, II 124–237.
[Useful on *Moralia*]
Plutarchos, Leipzig 1912.
[Particularly valuable for Plutarch's influence]

F. Leo, *Die griechisch-römische Biographie*, Leipzig 1901, 145–92.

C. P. Jones, *Plutarch and Rome*, Oxford 1971.
[The fullest and most recent treatment of Plutarch's life etc.]

R. M. Jones, *The Platonism of Plutarch*, Menasha, Wisconsin, 1916.
[Systematic and valuable]

J. Oakesmith, *The Religion of Plutarch*, London 1902.
[By an official of the G.P.O.; an amateur work in a good sense]

H. Peter, *Die Quellen Plutarchs in den Biographieen der Römer*, Halle 1865.

G. Soury, *La Démonologie de Plutarque*, Paris 1942.

R. Volkmann, *Leben, Schriften und Philosophie des Plutarch von Chaironeia,*
    Berlin 1869.
    [Still valuable]

K. Ziegler, 'Plutarchos', in Pauly-Wissowa, *Realenzyklopädie* . . . 1951
    (separately published 1949; revised 1964).
    [The standard, essential work of reference]

Index